RF

Contents

Cover: The war ended, but the scars remained: Galtié-Boissière's painting of the 'Parade of the War-wounded' in Paris, November 1918
Front endpaper: 'Everyone suddenly burst out singing'—jubilation in the streets of Paris on Armistice Day
Rear endpaper: 1934—the Leagues gather in preparation for the half-cock revolution of 6th February

First published in 1972 by Macdonald
St Giles House 49 Poland Street London W1
in the British Commonwealth and
American Heritage Press
Rockefeller Center New York
in the United States of America
Library of Congress Catalogue Card
Number: 78-37952 12-13-73
Made and printed in Great Britain by
Purnell & Sons Ltd Paulton Somerset

FRANCE: THE INSECURE PEACE

From Versailles to the Great Depression

J P T Bury

I should like to express my gratitude to my wife, who has typed virtually the whole of a difficult manuscript, and to Andrew Corbett, who has helped me at every stage in the preparation of this book.—
J.P.T.B.

Library of the 20th Century
Macdonald / American Heritage Press

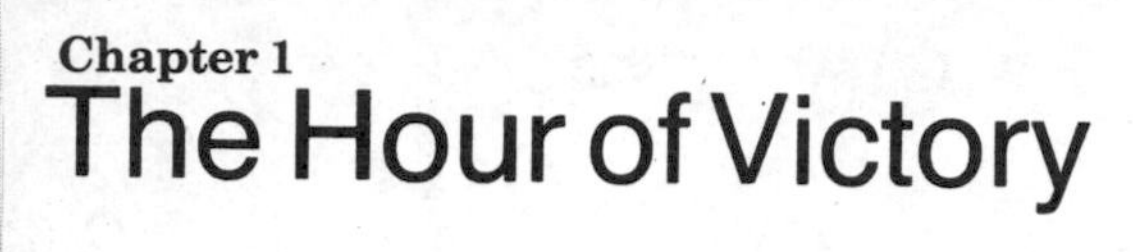

Chapter 1

The Hour of Victory

With the armistice of 11th November 1918, the First World War came to an end. It had involved the men and materials of almost every continent, but its principal battlefields had been European and much of the bloodiest fighting had taken place in France. Now Germany's dream of world domination was shattered. Against her had been arrayed the armies of the Allied and Associated Powers under the supreme command of a Frenchman, Marshal Foch. France, invaded in 1914, had occupied a pivotal place in the struggle. Defeated by a European coalition, including Prussia, in 1814 and 1815, defeated again by Prussia in 1870-1 and deprived of the two provinces of Alsace and Lorraine, she was now herself a leading member of a victorious coalition and had won the return match or *revanche* against her hereditary enemy across the Rhine.

The armistice terms were signed by Germany's delegates in Foch's railway carriage at Rethondes near Compiègne. The ensuing peace conference was held in Paris, the first such gathering in the city since 1856 when France was the foremost power on the continent. Conspicuous among the assembled statesmen was the septuagenarian French Prime Minister Clemenceau, 'the Tiger', who had assumed office in November 1917 and had rallied the spirits of a hard-pressed people. Now his countrymen gratefully hailed him as *'le Père la Victoire'*, the Father of Victory. It was in France too, in the glittering Hall of Mirrors of the Palace of Versailles, that the peace treaty with Germany was signed on 28th June 1919. In that same hall, forty-eight years earlier, Bismarck had proclaimed the German Empire which now lay in ruins. In Paris on 14th July, the anniversary of the fall of the Bastille, the traditional military review became a great victory parade of Allied troops along Napoleon's Avenue de la Grande Armée and under his Arc de Triomphe. These were some of the splendours of victory, and France was a focal point of

Left: *French troops enter Strasbourg in November 1918 to reclaim from Germany the 'lost provinces' of Alsace-Lorraine*

30

the great post-war celebrations. And when Foch and Clemenceau had visited London soon after the armistice, they were greeted enthusiastically as the men who had won the war. Their reception, said the British Prime Minister, Lloyd George, was 'such as I have never seen accorded to any foreign visitor'.

In France victory also meant celebrations of a more intimate character. On 11th November Clemenceau had read the armistice terms to the Chamber of Deputies. All those present had risen and sung the *Marseillaise* amid scenes of indescribable emotion. In a brief speech Clemenceau had declared that, with the help of those still living, France, 'once the soldier of God, today the soldier of humanity, and always the soldier of the ideal', would regain her place in the world and pursue her splendid course on the path of infinite human progress. She would do so, moreover, with the help of the people of her lost provinces. Already, on 4th November, he had been to Strasbourg in Alsace, to hail the recovery of that province and of Lorraine, and the French tricolour was flown again from the spire of its splendid cathedral. The visit was all the more moving because Clemenceau had been among those deputies who in 1871 had protested against their annexation. Soon afterwards the President of the French Republic, the Lorrainer Raymond Poincaré, conferred on the city the Legion of Honour for its heroism in war and under German occupation. The French university at Strasbourg was reinaugurated in his presence and hailed by a future President, Alexandre Millerand, as a bastion on the Rhine of those doctrines of liberty and civilisation which the heroic soldiers of the *Entente* had preserved from disaster. The recovery of the 'lost provinces' was the most treasured reward of victory. It meant the return of some 1,700,000 people who were so widely accepted as French that by international consensus there was no need to hold a plebiscite to determine their allegiance. It meant too the recovery of Lorraine's iron ore deposits and metallurgical works and of the textile factories and newly-developed potash mines of Upper Alsace. In addition, the treaty gave to France temporary ownership of the coal-mines of the adjacent Saarland. All these were substantial enrichments of her economy.

They were not her only territorial gains. Apart 11 ▷

Top left: *The victors were also the Peacemakers—(from left) Lloyd George, the Italian delegate Orlando, Clemenceau, and Woodrow Wilson.* ***Bottom:*** *Clemenceau presents the terms of the Versailles Treaty to the Chamber of Deputies, 30th June 1919. Many Frenchmen were still dissatisfied.* ***Next page:*** *War trophies litter the Place de la Concorde on Armistice Day 1918*

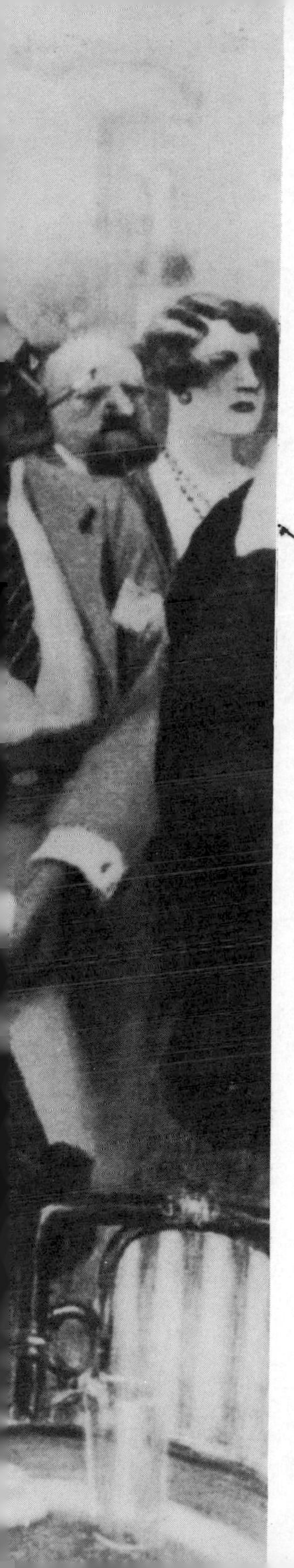

from guarantees in the Rhineland, France had not sought territory in Europe. But she was a colonial power, and naturally aspired to a share of the German colonial empire. Yet the stipulation by President Wilson in the celebrated Fourteen Points of the American peace programme that the interests of native populations should be considered ruled out direct annexation of colonial territories in pre-war style. Instead the Allies, who divided between them the control and administration of the former German colonies, did so as mandatory powers. The newly-formed League of Nations was given the title to the lands, and the mandatory powers were responsible to it for their administration. Under such terms France acquired Togoland and most of the Cameroons in West Africa, and the Syrian part of the former Ottoman Empire in the eastern Mediterranean.

Clemenceau's hopes for France's future seemed all the more likely to be realised because of changes in the balance of power. The Europe of 1919 was very different from the continent whose young men had marched joyfully to war in 1914. Then there had been three great empires east of the Rhine: Germany, Tsarist Russia, and Austria-Hungary. In 1919 there were none. The five great powers of the European mainland—Germany, Austria-Hungary, France, Russia, and Italy—had all been involved in the war. Only France and Italy had emerged undefeated.

Germany was prostrate and divided. The Weimar Republic, proclaimed in August 1919, was attacked from the Right by the army, which blamed the politicians for the defeat, and threatened from the Left by Communist revolution. Meanwhile, the military clauses of the peace treaty had reduced Germany to impotence. Her army was reduced to a volunteer force of 4,000 officers and 96,000 men, without tanks, aircraft, or offensive weapons. The General Staff, the War Academy, and the cadet schools were dissolved. The battle-fleet, scuttled by the Germans themselves at Scapa Flow, was to be replaced by a token force with no vessel larger than a small destroyer, and no submarines. An Allied Control Commission was appointed to supervise these disarmament measures.

If Germany was thus disarmed, her main ally, Austria-Hungary, no longer existed. The ancient empire of the Habsburgs had disintegrated into the five states of Austria, Hungary, Yugoslavia, Czechoslovakia, and Roumania, and the huge operation of liquidating the

Left: *While the Peace Conference settled the fate of Europe a mood of carefree indulgence swept Paris. André Guillaume's painting shows a typically cosmopolitan group in a music-hall foyer, popular haunt of men in search of girls of easy virtue*

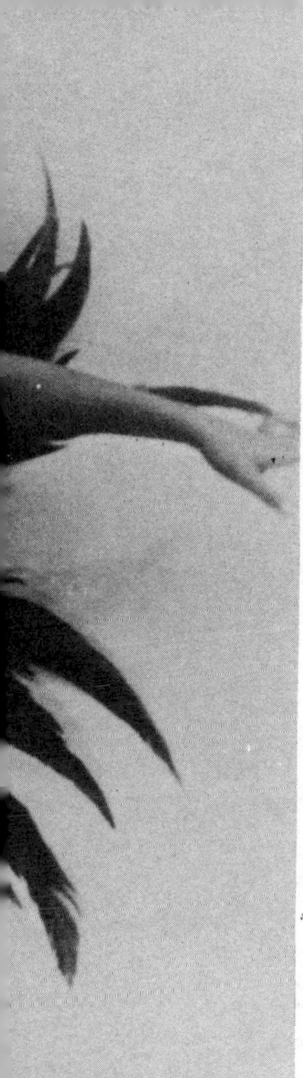

Austrian Empire was completed by the peace treaties.

Further east, France's former ally Russia was in the throes of the civil war which followed the Bolshevik coup of 1917. She was in a state of administrative and economic collapse. Ultimately it was only the obvious unacceptability of a return to Tsarist rule that gave the Bolshevik government at Moscow control of the whole country. After the failure of the dream of world-wide Communism, confidently predicted between 1917 and 1920, Soviet Russia was absorbed by her manifold internal problems. Reconstruction preoccupied her foremost leader, Lenin, until his death in 1924; when Stalin came to supreme power three years later the policy of isolation and retrenchment was consecrated in his slogan 'Socialism in one Country'.

Germany, Russia, and Austria had all suffered defeat, but Italy was on the winning side. However, she had been the weakest of the great powers. The burden of war had been heavy on her feebler natural and industrial resources, and the strain had engendered acute social unrest. In 1919 one and a half million workers occupied factories in north Italy, and brigandage was rife in the south. In 1922 the King offered Mussolini the premiership, and within two years Italian democracy was dead. But Italy remained militarily weak and economically backward. Although she competed for influence in Central Europe, she too was preoccupied with her own problems. She might be carping and critical, but she presented no serious threat to France.

So in 1919 France was supreme on the European continent and she remained so for the next decade. The British and the Americans had gone home to return to the relative isolation that had characterised their policies before the war. Germany was prostrate, Austria-Hungary dismembered, Russia anarchic and excluded from the councils of the West because of her aggressive opposition to the capitalist regimes which guided the rest of Europe. At the battle of Warsaw in 1920 it was with French help that the Poles halted the Bolshevik advance to world-wide revolution. Already by the end of 1921 France appeared so strong that the British Committee of Imperial Defence regarded her military superiority as 'overwhelming'. Whereas Germany 'could only under existing circumstances put into the field seven infantry divisions and three cavalry divisions fully armed and gunned', the Committee estimated that France had forty-four infantry and three cavalry divisions at home, and a further nineteen infantry and three cavalry divisions overseas. Also, Germany had 'no tanks and very few

Left: *Josephine Baker, Parisian cabaret idol of the twenties*

aeroplanes, while France has both in very large numbers'. As for the Russians, 'they have no army or equipment comparable in strength to Poland, Roumania, or Czechoslovakia'—all actual or future allies of France. Perhaps the most telling comment was that of the British High Command: 'We cannot contemplate a position where Great Britain would in a few years be at the mercy of France if present happy relations were to deteriorate'.

Paris: cultural queen

The hegemony that France thus appeared to exercise in the political world she also unquestionably enjoyed in many realms of culture. Paris was still the *Ville Lumière,* the City of Enlightenment, the Mecca of artists and men of letters, the town in which cultured Americans wished to die. In 1919 the French literary scene was dominated by four illustrious figures. These were the versatile novelist, essayist, and traveller André Gide, who emphasised the multiplicity of truth and was to champion African natives and flirt with Communism, the exquisite dilettante Marcel Proust, whose ill-health turned him into a recluse exploring the stream of consciousness and in his darkened room writing his great work *A la Recherche du Temps Perdu,* and the poets Paul Valéry and Paul Claudel, the latter a Roman Catholic who also achieved high rank as a diplomat. In addition, there was a host of other writers who gave distinction to the post-war decades and gained a reputation which spread far beyond France's frontiers. They included Roger Martin du Gard and Georges Duhamel, who were the French counterparts of John Galsworthy and his *Forsyte Saga,* André Maurois, the biographer of Shelley and author of the witty *Silences du Colonel Bramble,* Julien Green who wrote powerful and terrifying novels such as *Adrienne Mesurat,* and André Malraux, General de Gaulle's future Minister of Culture, whose harsh world of oriental adventure was to be portrayed in *La Condition Humaine.* Most sparkling of all, though not the most profound, was Jean Cocteau, a dazzling butterfly who experimented with many kinds of art, with ballets and films as well as with poetry, drama, and the novel.

Nor were these all. Crowds flocked to the theatre to see the delightful and witty comedies of Sacha Guitry, a superb entertainer, and of Marius Pagnol, while the

Right: *'A place and a time without equal in the history of the world'—so the writer Jules Romains described Paris in the twenties. The literary reputations of André Gide* **(top left)** *and Marcel Proust, d. 1922* **(top right),** *flourished amidst the talents of a younger generation—men like the American artist Man Ray (left of the group,* **bottom***) and poet Ezra Pound (standing fourth from left) and the mercurial Jean Cocteau (seated right)*

brilliant, more serious Jean Giraudoux was fortunate in having the greatest actor of the day, Louis Jouvet, as his interpreter. They flocked, too, to the music halls, to see an old favourite, Mistinguett, and a new star, Maurice Chevalier, while those who went to night-clubs adored the negress dancer, Josephine Baker, whose spell reflected the new vogue for things African. As for music lovers, they could enjoy the wit and polish of Maurice Ravel, and the compositions in many keys at once of 'The Six', a group which soon broke up but some of whose members individually commanded a great reputation and attracted the younger generation searching for novelty. Another undeniable influence on musical development was Igor Stravinsky, one of so many foreigners whose spiritual home was Paris.

Poets abounded also and here, in particular, as in painting and the visual arts generally, the movement known as Surrealism was a widespread influence. Already before 1914 the traditional patterns in literature and art had been disturbed by revolutionary movements which glorified dynamism, scorned representational art, and rejected conventional values. They had created a new climate of intellectual discontent and now their disturbing influence was reinforced by that of the great Austrian psychologist Freud and his explorations of the subconscious. So it was that the Surrealist group, led by André Breton, launched their first manifesto in 1924, calling upon man to look for the source of poetic imagination in the subconscious and to seek his inspiration in dreams and the twilight world of shifting impulses and obscure desires rooted in sexual instincts. The Surrealists' influence impelled poets and other artists to invest ordinary and unrelated words and objects with a peculiar significance and their revolutionary approach provoked a stirring revival of the perennial debate about the nature of poetry and art. At the same time, while many writers between the wars were escapist and turned their backs on contemporary problems, the Surrealists were in general strongly Left-wing in their political sympathies; they were anti-militarist, anti-capitalist, and anticlerical. Arrayed against them were a number of Catholic

Right: *Pre-war themes continued for a time to fertilise painting styles—the Futurist 'Nude descending a staircase' was painted by Duchamp in 1912, and 'Tea' by Matisse in 1919* ***(next page).*** *A new movement, known as Surrealism, expressed more of the growing uncertainties of the post-war age. It aimed to free the imagination from the restraints of reason and society by plotting with disturbing realism the images of the subconscious and the irrational world of dream. Its most sensational exponent in the field of painting was Salvador Dali; his 'Triangular hour' (1933)* ***(page 20)*** *details the inexplicable*

writers, such as the philosopher Jacques Maritain, who exercised great influence in intellectual circles and 'sought for springs more refreshing than those that flowed from Marx or welled up from the "libido" at the call of Freud'. Maritain's home at Meudon became an intellectual centre of international repute.

Paris, so long a cosmopolitan city, had particularly attracted painters and sculptors, and in this respect she was still unrivalled. To her, between the wars, returned such painters as the Italian Modigliani, the Russian Marc Chagall, and, towering above and, in the end, outliving them all, the Spaniard Pablo Picasso. In Paris also two of the most influential sculptors of the age, the Roumanian Brancusi and the Swiss Giacometti, did much of their greatest work. Apart from these foreigners, there were, of course, great French painters still alive, men like Braque and Matisse, whose reputations were already established. Such men continued to paint remarkable and sensitive pictures which hung easily in the atmosphere of elegant drawing-rooms. But the more disquieting works of others fitted less happily into such surroundings. Such pictures also reflected the influence of Surrealism and its search for the subconscious. Thus the versatile Picasso passed from an 'antique' phase into a Surrealist one, and after 1925 he painted a series of deformed portraits, monstrous figures which seemed to typify a universe which had run amok.

Here indeed was the rub. The intellectual ferment reflected the profound disarray and rejection of established values which followed the Great War and which was not confined to France but was a widespread phenomenon in the Western world. But it was this rejection which appealed to many of the younger generation in France and it was matched by many less intellectual discontents in French society. These increased as time went on. The great military victory had its miseries as well as its splendours. And these miseries contributed not a little to political and social frustrations.

Chapter 2

Counting the Cost

The victory of 1918 was splendid, but it had been won at a terrible price. Armistice Day had seen untold rejoicing, but its anniversary would be observed in France, as elsewhere, as a day of solemn remembrance of a generation killed in the war. For France the toll was crushing. Almost every family was in mourning—'The élite of her youth,' as Clemenceau put it, 'was at rest in a shroud of glory.' 1,390,000 men, the equivalent of ten per cent of the active male population, were dead or missing. Their memory would be preserved in innumerable war memorials and in great cemeteries amid what was once the nightmare landscape of the battlefields. For the countless soldiers who had perished unknown there was a special monument. To honour them all, one of them was interred beneath the great Arc de Triomphe in Paris. The Tomb of the Unknown Soldier was and is guarded by an undying flame.

In addition to the dead and missing, 740,000 men had been maimed, many so badly that they were unfit for any kind of work. They survived as living witnesses to the greatest holocaust in history. The state did its best to care for them, to give them and their dependants pensions, and to find suitable employment for those still capable of working. The seats reserved for the *'mutilés de la guerre'* on buses and trains and on the Paris underground were one small visible indication of this care and a constant reminder to Frenchmen and tourists alike of the cost of war in human suffering.

These devastating losses had serious consequences. For one thing, the death rate among officers had been higher than that in the ranks. The ablest young men had paid a heavier toll and the country was impoverished accordingly. For another, before the war France's population had already been increasing more slowly and had a larger proportion of old people than that of any other great power. The war resulted in a further ageing of the population: there was a sharp decline in

Left: *The casualties of war parade through Paris. France's aim now was 'to win the peace'—and cripple Germany*

the birth rate since so many young men were away fighting—one historian has estimated that in 1915 alone 1,600,000 potential births were lost. No sooner was it over than it was followed by a virulent influenza epidemic which claimed 200,000 victims. The recovery of 1,700,000 Alsatians and Lorrainers was no adequate counter to cumulative mortality on such a scale.

All the main European belligerents had suffered immense casualties, yet France's were the greatest in proportion to her total population. Moreover, Germany, in spite of her defeat and losses of territory, kept her demographic superiority. In 1921 France's population numbered only 39,200,000, whereas that of Germany was more than 60,000,000. France's relative poverty in manpower might sooner or later be a serious weakness. Meanwhile, to make up for her losses she had more than ever to supplement her labour force with foreign immigrants.

France had also suffered immense material damage, unlike Germany which was virtually unscathed because the war had been mainly fought beyond her frontiers. For most of the time the north-eastern departments of France, which included some of her richest agricultural land and her main mining and industrial areas, had been occupied by the enemy or provided the great battlefields of the Western Front. 352,000 houses had been destroyed or badly damaged and 3,000,000 acres had been rendered unfit for cultivation. The loss of livestock was enormous. 62,000 kilometres of roads had to be remade as well as some 5,000 kilometres of railway and nearly 2,000 of canals. Output in devastated and flooded coal fields had fallen to forty per cent and overall industrial production to sixty per cent of the levels in 1914. Moreover, there were other significant losses: for instance, the merchant marine had lost twenty-five per cent of its tonnage. In consequence, one of the stipulations in the armistice and the peace treaty which had unanimous support from public opinion was the requirement that Germany should pay full compensation for the destruction wrought in the war she was accused of starting. Frenchmen believed that they had a 'sacred right' to reparation. Unfortunately, all the other Allies also claimed their share. The reparations question was to be one of the most intricate and contentious in international politics during the coming decade.

For a century France had been remarkable for financial buoyancy. The franc had been 'solid as a rock', she had regularly balanced her budgets and, despite many proposals, she had not thought it necessary to make any

Left: *War-ravaged Rheims. Germany's 'war guilt' hardened French determination that she should pay the bill in full*

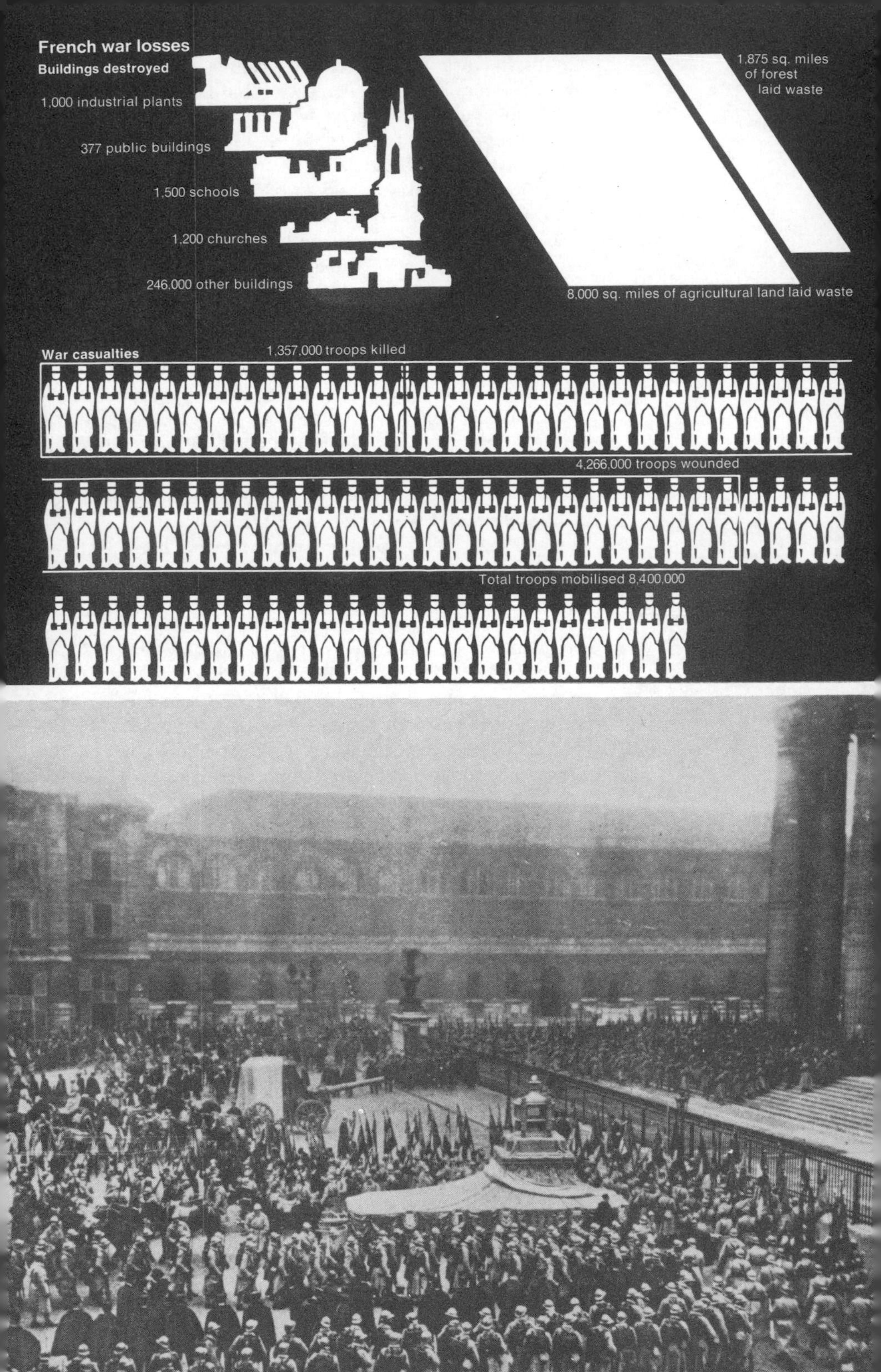

French war losses
Buildings destroyed
1,000 industrial plants
377 public buildings
1,500 schools
1,200 churches
246,000 other buildings
1,875 sq. miles of forest laid waste
8,000 sq. miles of agricultural land laid waste
War casualties
1,357,000 troops killed
4,266,000 troops wounded
Total troops mobilised 8,400,000

radical changes in her old-fashioned tax structure which depended over-much on indirect taxes. The only considerable innovation had been the introduction in 1916 of an income tax. But this left many loopholes and its low rates meant that what elsewhere was a main source of revenue accounted in France for only a quarter of the total raised from taxes. Now the picture was fundamentally altered. She was saddled with a public debt which had increased more than six-fold. Her governments had borrowed great sums both from the Bank of France and from the public in the form of short-term defence bonds. She had also had to make considerable purchases abroad and to borrow overseas, especially from the United States. In addition, as a result of the Bolshevik Revolution, she lost the large sums she had invested in Russia, for the revolutionary government, treated more or less as an outlaw by the Western powers, would not honour Tsarist debts or offer compensation. France was faced by the new and endemic problem of financial instability, by the question of war debts (which also bedevilled international relations), and by growing inflation. Rising prices and living costs were widespread in Europe but this did not make them easier to bear. Frenchmen resented such bitter fruits of victory and were all the more eager to exact the utmost in reparation.

The battle to win the peace

Her great losses in the war had been largely due to France's vulnerability. So from the outset in 1918, dominating the whole business of peace-making so far as France was concerned, was another problem – security. She had now been invaded three times in a century and at the end of 1918 Frenchmen wanted nothing so much as to feel that they would never again be the victims of German aggression.

'We have won the war,' said Clemenceau, 'we must win the peace. This will be still more difficult.' And so it proved. The business of peace-making was protracted, arduous, and complicated. It involved clashes of personality, clashes between idealists and realists, and clashes of national interests. The cause of French recovery was in the hands of an old man of seventy-eight who had recently blithely recovered from being wounded in the shoulder by an anarchist.

Clemenceau – tough, cynical, disillusioned, a man of few but telling words – was essentially a realist. He had

***Left:** The terrible toll of devastation **(top)**, and a tribute to the memory of the countless dead **(bottom)** – the coffin of the Unknown Soldier enters the Panthéon, 11th November 1920, before going to its final resting-place beneath the Arc de Triomphe*

to contend mainly with the British and American leaders, for Orlando, the Italian, played only a minor part, except where Italian interests were directly concerned. The American President, Woodrow Wilson, the only head of state to take part in the peace conference, was a lofty idealist 'who believed in mankind but distrusted all men'. He had come to bestow his preconceived ideas and principles upon the Old World, but it would not be so easy to fit them to the intensely complex realities of European politics. The British Prime Minister, Lloyd George, had no such high ideals. He was a canny Welshman, charming, agile in debate, and infinitely supple and sensitive to the gusts of public opinion at home. He was traditionally concerned with British trade interests and the European balance of power. The first meant, among other things, speedy European, including German, economic recovery; the second that the balance should not be tilted too strongly in favour of any one power, meaning, in present circumstances, France.

The conditions which French nationalists thought necessary to protect their country would have made radical changes in the government and character of much of the historic and oft-contested borderlands on France's eastern frontier. Clemenceau had originally demanded the return of the greater part of the Saar territory which had belonged to France for nearly a quarter of a century in the Revolutionary and Napoleonic period. But he had been unsuccessful. The historical justification was flimsy, the people were indisputably German in sympathy, and Wilson and Lloyd George were both adamant in their opposition to the creation of 'a new Alsace-Lorraine in reverse'. Clemenceau had to be content, as has been seen, with control of the coalmines and separation of the territory from Germany for fifteen years under League of Nations administration. This was a first, but minor, setback.

Much more important were the demands already put forward by Marshal Foch in two notes of 27th November 1918 and 19th January 1919. He required, in particular, two things: the permanent military occupation of the Rhineland and its political separation from the rest of Germany in such a way as to form one or two separate states. But once more France's proposals came up against firm opposition from Wilson and Lloyd George. Wilson was the apostle of national self-determination. How could he impose political separation on the Rhinelanders if they did not want it? Lloyd George, moreover, feared that a Rhineland buffer state must inevitably be the

Left: *The opening in 1927 of the massive Douaumont Cemetery. France slept uneasily while her eastern border stayed insecure*

pawn of France and tilt the balance of power unduly in French favour.

Clemenceau recognised that he could not win political separation, but he fought stubbornly to secure permanent military occupation. In consequence Wilson and Lloyd George came back with a counter offer. Since France feared for her eastern frontier, the United States and Great Britain would guarantee her security by each concluding with her a treaty whereby they would come to her aid if she were again attacked by Germany. But the British guarantee would be effective only if the American one were ratified by the US Congress.

Very reluctantly Clemenceau gave way. To the anger of Foch and his nationalist supporters he accepted this compromise and dropped the idea of a buffer state. But he still insisted that there should be a military occupation of the Rhineland, if not permanently, at least for a term of years. In consequence the area, together with certain bridgeheads across the river, was divided into three zones, one of which might be evacuated at the end of each five years provided that Germany honoured her treaty obligations. The maximum period of occupation for any one zone was to be fifteen years. But Clemenceau reckoned that Germany would be sure to default and that the period could then be prolonged.

The terms of the treaty were communicated to the German delegates in a brief grim speech by Clemenceau on 7th May. They had not been allowed to negotiate and for six weeks it was doubtful whether the German government would accept conditions which they regarded as a *Diktat* (ultimatum). During that period Lloyd George tried to secure substantial modifications. But Wilson supported Clemenceau in standing firm. The changes made in this interval were minor and the Allies were ready to invade Germany if the treaty were rejected. A government crisis ensued in Germany and eventually a new cabinet agreed to accept it. A few minutes after 3 pm on 28th June 1919 the German plenipotentiaries affixed their signature to the vast treaty of 440 articles. It was five years to the day since the assassination of the Archduke Franz Ferdinand at Sarajevo – the immediate cause of what everyone now called 'the Great War'.

The Treaty of Versailles was a great and elaborate settlement, but it left many dissatisfied, as did the other treaties which completed the peace-making. The Germans resented not only the way in which the terms had been dictated to them, but many of the provisions, especially

Top right: *President Poincaré, himself a Lorrainer, tours newly recovered Lorraine. 'Now I can die,' he said. But further trials awaited him.* ***Bottom:*** *The French occupation of Koblenz, 1919*

The Tiger: **" Curious! I seem to hear a child we**

the so-called war-guilt clause (Article 231) which forced them to accept responsibility for the outbreak of war, the provisions for the trial of so-called war criminals, and those which delineated the new eastern frontier which meant the transfer of much territory to a resuscitated Poland. The Italians were discontented because their territorial ambitions were not fully met, and in France, when the treaty came before parliament for ratification, Clemenceau was the target of bitter attacks. The Versailles settlement was denounced as 'Wilson's peace' and for many on the Right the *Père la Victoire* had become '*perd la victoire*', the man who loses the victory. Clemenceau, the critics said, had failed to divide Germany, he had failed to secure the Rhine frontier and the Saar, and he had allowed the French claims to reparation to be whittled away. Moreover, what, they asked, was the worth of the American and British guarantees unsupported by specific military commitments? As for Foch, when he heard of the signing he had, as Winston Churchill was to record, 'observed with singular accuracy: "This is not peace. It is an armistice".'

The question of guarantees was indeed a crucial one. The guarantees presupposed ratification of the treaty by the United States. But Wilson had mishandled the situation at home and there was growing opposition to the treaty. Then in September he had a stroke; in March 1920 ratification was rejected by the Senate. The main corner-stone of Clemenceau's edifice of security was knocked away. At the end of the debate in the Chamber he had told the deputies that what they were about to vote on was 'not even a beginning, but the beginning of a beginning' and he agreed that France must still be condemned to eternal vigilance. After March 1920 the beginning of the beginning would be all the more arduous and the price of vigilance all the more exacting.

Left: *One of the most prophetic cartoons of all time, by Englishman Will Dyson—as Clemenceau leaves the Peace Conference he hears the sound of a young child weeping. The Treaty contained the seeds of destruction for the next generation*

Chapter 3

Society and Politics

The Germans had a saying that it was good to live like God in France. To many outsiders France before the war had seemed an enviable land in which a large number of people contrived to live cheaply and well. A great diversity of products came from her three distinct climatic regions, whose variety added to her charm: the Mediterranean area, the mountain districts, and the oceanic belt of the west and north. She was nearly self-sufficient in food production, she grew more wheat than any European country save Russia, and her wines were unrivalled. Agriculture was her greatest industry, but industrialisation had made great strides since the mid-19th century. It had, however, proceeded less rapidly than in Britain, Germany, and Belgium and, although she had abundance of iron ore and bauxite, she was poor in such basic raw material for heavy industry as good coking coal. But this slower development had meant that the social problems attendant upon industrialisation had been less formidable than elsewhere. Her manufacturers had concentrated largely on the home market and, although they still produced for export the luxury goods for which France was famous, there was no general compulsion to export or die. Her form of government was a democratic republic, now accepted by the great majority of Frenchmen. The property-owning democracy which was the ideal of many French revolutionaries had, to a considerable extent, been achieved, and the slogan 'Liberty, Equality, and Fraternity' was no empty catchword. Frenchmen enjoyed much political freedom; the principle of equality of opportunity had long been established and French society was remarkably free from snobbery and colour prejudice.

But France in 1919-20 was still essentially a land of 'small men' and small units, a land with a social and political structure which reflected a fierce individualism and a deep attachment to the family and the soil. This individualism was echoed in an old saying: 'My glass is small but it is my own glass that I drink from.'

Left: *The backbone of France—a traditional peasant family*

At the bottom of the social structure the peasantry had for centuries been regarded as the backbone of the country. The war had shown how true this was. 3,700,000 of them had been mobilised, nearly 700,000 had been killed and 400,000 were too badly maimed to work again. Many of the survivors were embittered, and this boded ill for the future. Yet, though their ranks were terribly depleted and although migration to the towns increased (the agricultural population declined from 7,800,000 in 1919 to 6,730,000 in 1931), cultivation of the soil was still the principal occupation. As late as 1939 more than fifty-five per cent of the population lived in places with less than 4,000 inhabitants. More than half the peasant farmers and their womenfolk worked their own lands, one-third were tenants, and the remainder share croppers or labourers. But the average size of a farm was no more than thirty-six acres and many were scattered as well as small. A plan was indeed proposed in 1920 by Pierre Caziot, a future Minister of Agriculture in the Vichy regime, to regroup holdings which were too small and divide big ones into 'family-size units', but it came to nothing. Under these circumstances mechanisation was only beginning to appear; few could afford it, the size of many farms was too small to encourage it, and the peasant tended to be conservative and slow to adopt new tools and techniques. By 1939 the number of tractors did not exceed 30,000. In addition, living conditions were often primitive. Electricity, indeed, was rapidly being extended to remote districts, but even in the 1960s it was reckoned that seventy-five per cent of peasant farmers' dwellings had no running water. To observers in countries where land-holding was less fragmented and mechanisation more advanced, the continuance of the small man and the small unit denoted an agriculture that was backward and inefficient. One critic would remark that if the French economy died it would be found with a pitchfork through its heart.

The small man on the land had his counterpart in factories and shops. Of course heavy industry existed and big concerns in the Paris region and elsewhere employed thousands of men. The war had both shifted some of the centres of heavy industry and given an impetus to industrialisation generally. But it was the small business which still dominated the scene. In 1931 sixty per cent

Right: *While agricultural France pursued its timeless way of life the cosmopolitan capital cherished the daring and the exotic. Mistinguett was one of the best-known cabaret artistes at the famous Casino de Paris.* ***Next page:*** *'Dancing' (1925), by Vertés.* ***Page 40:*** *1925 cabaret poster advertises a special attraction. In the diversity and Bohemian freedom of Parisian social life talented American Negroes could breathe more easily*

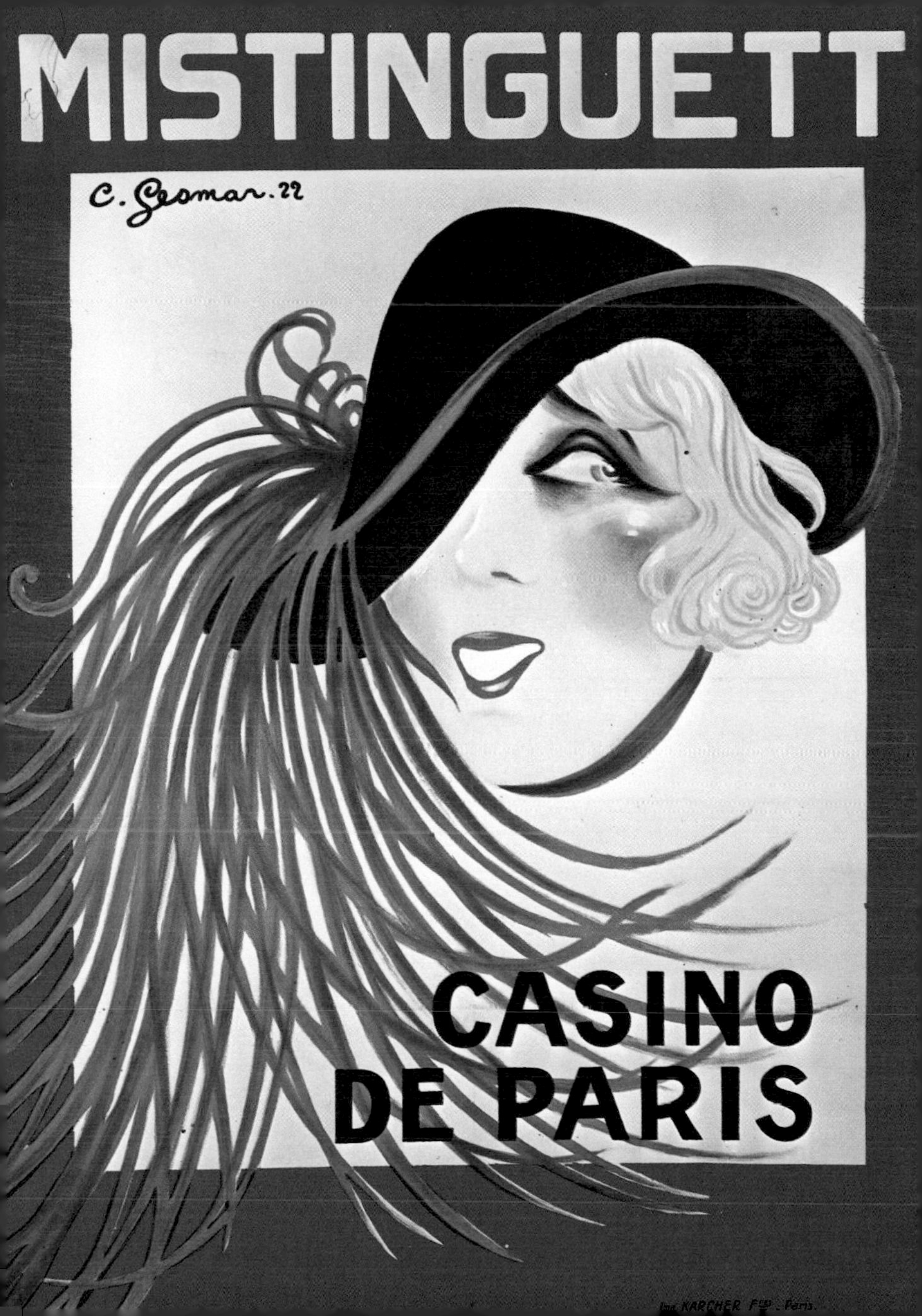

MISTINGUETT

C. Gesmar. 22

CASINO DE PARIS

Imp. KARCHER Fres. Paris.

LA
REVUE NÈGRE
AU
PAUL COLIN
Music-hall
DES
CHAMPS-ÉLYSÉES
H. CHACHOIN Imp. PARIS - 1925

of France's workers were employed in firms of fewer than twenty people. The artisan, with his tradition of fine craftsmanship, was still very much alive and a vast number of employers continued to have close personal relationships with their men. France had largely escaped 'that semi-mystical intoxication' with production which obsessed the Anglo-Saxon world and made it more dynamic economically, though not necessarily a more human or gracious world in which to live. Alongside the artisan there were countless other small men in the towns. For the most part they ranked among the 'petite bourgeoisie' or lowest strata in the infinitely graded and overlapping series of groups which comprised the middle classes. In their politics it was said that they wore their hearts on the Left, but kept their wallets on the Right, and in general they accepted the standards and aspirations of the middle and upper classes who dominated the scene and in whom the former aristocracy had largely merged. At the top were the 'haute bourgeoisie', whom a writer in the 1880s described as consisting of 'rich families, the leading members of the liberal professions, important landowners, financiers and industrialists'. The description still held good, and the industrialists, in particular, had organised into powerful political pressure groups which threw their weight behind the Right.

If the haute bourgeoisie were at the top, so Paris was at the centre, 'the heart and brain of the country', and more than ever dominant. There were many splendid provincial cities but Paris was unique, the cultural and political capital, the pivot of the railway system, the centre of an industrialised area, the magnet which drew ambitious young men from the provinces. In and around Paris were enshrined the most sacred memorials of a history to which another great page had just been added.

Yet although Paris was the seat of government, it did not dominate the French press or set the political tone. The provinces had flourishing newspapers of their own and it was they who imparted a peculiar flavour to the nation's politics. The political heart of the country beat in the cafés of innumerable small towns and in the electoral committees and political huddles of the local notables. They were the men whom the deputies courted and whose interests they fostered. To one brilliant writer the republic was essentially a 'Republic of Committees'. These notables were small men and individualists and their horizons were often limited, but it was they who counted. They helped to give the regime its peculiarly negative character.

The political framework of the Third Republic

The Third Republic existed as a compromise; it was the form of government that divided Frenchmen least. The constitution had aimed at a balance between the executive and the legislature, and the President of the Republic had been given power to dissolve the Chamber of Deputies. But this power had fallen into disuse. The President of the Republic was elected for seven years, but since 1879 he had seldom been more than a politician of average ability. Poincaré, President since 1913, was an exception, but he was due to retire in January 1920. Thus parliament was supreme.

It consisted of two houses, an upper house or Senate of men of forty and over, elected for nine years by a heterogeneous collection of local notables, and a lower house, the Chamber. The Senate, like all upper houses, was intended to act as a brake upon hasty legislation. It performed this function with watchful and sometimes reactionary zeal. Thus it had for decades delayed the introduction of an income tax and it still frowned upon votes for women – the world of politics continued to be a male one, despite the social emancipation of women resulting from the war. The Chamber was elected for four years and, since it was virtually immune from dissolution, the deputies were free during that time to make and unmake ministries and give their own peculiar rendering of democratic rule. All parliaments tend to be more or less agreeable clubs in which the members look after their own interests as well as those of their friends and electors, but to a genial contemporary satirist the French deputies seemed peculiarly concerned with patronage: it was a 'Republic of Pals' as well as a 'Republic of Committees'.

This republic was notorious for its ministerial instability – there had been sixty-two cabinets between 1870 and 1913 – and many attributed this to the irresponsibility of deputies free from the threat of dissolution. But the fundamental reason lay in the party system. Many Frenchmen had envied the English two-party system, but attempts to develop it in France had never succeeded. French politicians were too individualist and so France, like many other countries, had several parties. In 1918, broadly speaking, there were three main groupings: conservatives with various labels on the Right, Radicals and Radical-Socialists in the Centre, and Socialists on the Left. Outside parliament, and despising it, was the neo-monarchist party, the *Action Française*, whose members pledged themselves to fight every re-

Top right: *Parallel methods of cultivation, the ox and the tractor.*
Bottom: *Political nerve-centre of France – the provincial café*

CAFÉ.HÔTEL DU COMMERCE
CAFÉ ET HÔTEL DU COMMERCE

publican regime. Apart from the *Action Française* and the Socialists (and, later, the Communists), French parties were not disciplined, highly-organised, bodies. Many indeed were little more than groupings of electoral committees, whose main objects were to devise election programmes and support particular candidates. Loosely organised in the country as a whole, they were no more subject to strict discipline in parliament. Deputies and senators were indeed enrolled in groups, but these were not the same in each house nor, except on the Left, did they necessarily correspond to the parties outside parliament. In consequence, deputies enrolled in one group might belong to different parties, just as members of different groups might belong to the same party. In general, in the words of a French party analyst, there was 'no discipline either in the party or the group'.

In these circumstances all ministries tended to be coalitions of shifting groups, in which many of the same men reappeared, and all coalitions tended to include the Radicals, who were strategically placed in the centre of the spectrum.

French democracy had three further characteristics which emphasised its negative character. It had originated with the French Revolution, which had been regarded as advancing ever further towards the Left. Thus, for those who accepted the Revolution, the path of 'Progress' lay to the Left. As André Siegfried wrote, French democracy was 'a movement' in which programmes were less important than relative positions: you must always be on your enemy's Left—'always on the Left, but no further'. Secondly, Frenchmen had such a passion for discussing principles that the wording of a motion often seemed more important than the legislation to which it referred. Thirdly, those who accepted the Revolution so distrusted power and its corrupting possibilities that they tended to confuse strong with reactionary government. The small man, of whom the Radicals were the prime representatives, was more concerned to keep watch on those who had power than to press them to initiate reform. Moreover, since coalition governments tended to be divided about important reforms, the easiest course was generally to shelve them.

Democracy is a rambling house of many mansions, but the French mansion was indeed paradoxical. In the words of one writer, it was a regime that was 'conservative in purse, revolutionary at heart; extremist and idealist in its programmes, opportunist and moderate in action; admiring great men but refusing them power; captivated by eloquence and words, but freely changing its orators'.

Bismarck, Clemenceau once reminded the deputies, had thought that the republic would be weak: 'Well,'

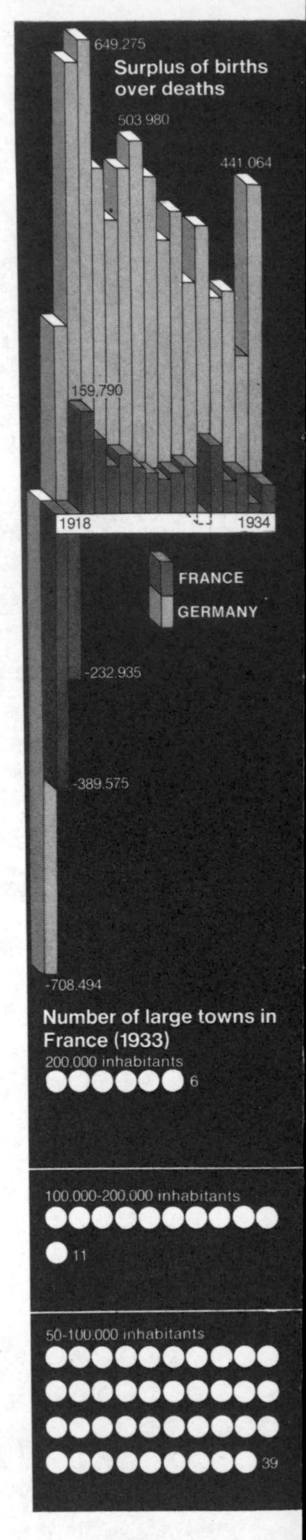

commented Clemenceau, 'the experiment . . . has been able to develop freely for half a century.' The implication was, why not for another half century? Yet this development had taken place in an era when the best government still tended to be regarded as that which governed least. The balance between executive and legislature had been tilted so firmly in favour of the legislature that the executive was faced by an almost impenetrable obstacle-course if it wished to institute reform. The weakness of the presidency, the last-ditch conservatism of the Senate, the precariousness of ministries, and the kaleidoscopic party pattern all contributed to a system in which the buck of responsibility could be effortlessly passed and in which the inertia of vested interests was the strongest force. Many aspects of French life had been drastically changed by the war; but the system of government remained obstinately the same. Aptly, the Palais Bourbon, where the Chamber met, had no windows looking outwards. Might not its inmates, playing the old parliamentary games in the old traditional ways, be living in too closed an atmosphere, one ill-fitted for the resolution of the problems of the post-war age? Indeed perhaps the greatest of these problems was whether, without sacrificing liberty and relapsing into dictatorship, France could adjust her system of government to meet the needs of the modern world.

The domestic problems of peace

The transition from war to peace is never easy. Men are impatient to return to pre-war conditions and then find that these cannot be restored; they react impetuously against war-time disciplines and their mood is often rebellious. In France after 1918 the transition was smoother than in some other countries. Demobilisation was completed within a year of the armistice. War-time ministries and special services were wound up. Requisitioned railways were handed back to their owners. Unemployment, which rose to great heights elsewhere, was mitigated because there was an immense work of reconstruction to be done and because working hours were reduced from a norm of nine or ten hours to eight in April 1919.

The war had accelerated changes in working conditions which were not to the workers' advantage. For the first time there were more metallurgical than textile workers. Concentration of industry had increased and the growth of mass-production methods in big industries,

Left: *The balance between rural and urban populations remained reasonably constant in France, but the gap between the populations of France and Germany continued to widen*

C.G.T.
PARIS
CHARCUTERIE

such as those which made cars and aeroplanes, turned many of the workers into mere cogs in a machine, while their employment became more precarious. In France, as elsewhere, there had been scandals about war profiteers and 'nouveaux riches'. The political sympathies of the '*métallos*' and many other workers in heavy industry were far to the Left, and in the Paris industrial region the peripheral districts where many of them lived became known as '*la banlieue rouge*', the red suburbs.

But the government was not unfriendly to the workers. In March 1919 a law was passed legalising collective bargaining and in April the eight-hour day, one of the major demands of the pre-war workers' movements, was conceded. Soon afterwards, however, the climate deteriorated. The government, fearing disturbances, banned a great May Day demonstration. The ban was defied and in clashes with the police one man was killed and several were wounded. A month later there was a violent strike of Paris metal-workers. It was the prelude to a series of industrial disturbances which reached their height in 1920, and to a trial of strength between the French trade union organisations and the state.

The main workers' organisation, the CGT (*Confédération Générale du Travail*), had been split by the war, but when victory came it closed its ranks and put forward a minimum programme of reform. This included the nationalisation of various industries and a number of other demands. The laws of March and April 1919 went only part of the way towards meeting them. It looked as though the workers would have to await the election of a Left-wing government to obtain further concessions. But the elections of November 1919 brought in the Right, not the Left. Although the Socialists won twenty-three per cent of the votes they gained only eleven per cent of the seats in the Chamber. The Radicals also lost many seats. This was a bitter disappointment. Meanwhile, Communist propaganda increased and the whole situation was aggravated by continuing inflation in which a steady rise in the cost of living was not matched by wage increases. As a result, by the end of the war real wages had fallen below the 1914 level. Everyone complained of the high cost of living, '*la vie chère*'. Trade union numbers, always liable to fluctuation, soared to above two million in 1920 (about one third of the whole industrial labour force), and the small Catholic unions united in 1919 to form the CFTC *(Confédération Française des Travailleurs Chrétiens)*, which soon boasted more than 100,000 members. There was a sharp renewal of strikes in 1919, which ex-

Left: *Members of the leading trade union organisation, the CGT, demonstrate in April 1919: war had aggravated grievances*

PARTI SOCIALIS
SECTION FRANÇAISE DE L'INTERNATIONALE
PROLÉTAIRES DE TOUS PAYS UNISSEZ

tended still further in 1920: railway-workers, dockers, miners, metal and building workers all came out. But when the CGT hoped to achieve the old dream of French revolutionary syndicalists or unionists and bring the state to its knees by a general strike, it failed. The government refused to be intimidated. It would not negotiate until the strikers returned to work. It prosecuted the CGT for conspiring against the state, and it arrested the secretary of the railwaymen's union. The failure meant bitter disillusionment for the workers and contributed to schism both in the Socialist Party and the unions themselves. As a vivid indicator of frustration union membership rapidly fell to 600,000. Many new recruits thought twice about paying their hard-earned centimes to an organisation which had failed to secure results.

The schisms were momentous. The doctrinaire individualism of the Frenchman had been clearly illustrated in the earlier history of French socialism and it was not until 1905 that the numerous socialist groups had become unified in a single party. Now the impact of Russian Communism rent asunder this hard-won unity. At the Socialist Party congress at Tours in 1920 there was a bitter clash between moderates and extremists. The moderates accepted the peace settlement, remained loyal to the Second International, and were still ready to work through parliament. The extremists denounced the peace treaties as capitalist instruments forged to maintain bourgeois dominance, and they looked to Russia, the one example of victorious social revolution. They were impatient with those who thought that anything could be gained through parliament, and in the frustrated mood of 1920 it was they and the magic of Soviet power which carried the day. They were the majority and they left the Socialists and formed the French Communist Party, taking with them the well-known paper *L'Humanité* and a large number of trade unionists who set up a rival union to the CGT. This was known as the CGTU *(Confédération Générale du Travail Unitaire)*. It was affiliated to the Moscow Profintern and drew its strength mainly from railwaymen, builders, and metal workers in the Paris region. A new, disciplined party thus appeared in France to the Left of the Socialists. What was particularly ominous was that it took its orders from an organisation in Moscow, the Third International, which was patently controlled by a foreign power.

Victory for the *Bloc National*

The Left was thus weakened and the workers were

***Left:** Socialist Party delegates at the 1920 Tours Congress, which spawned the Moscow-controlled French Communist Party* thrust back on the defensive. Meanwhile, for the first time since the 1870s, a Right-wing Chamber had been elected. The voters had turned out in strength – they were men, of course, for women were not given the vote until 1944 – and the new system had told in favour of the more disciplined parties. The result had been a sweeping victory for the union of conservative groups known as the *Bloc National*. As most of the new deputies were ex-servicemen, the new chamber was dubbed the *'Chambre Bleu Horizon'*, from the colour of French uniforms. Its election was the counterpart of the khaki election in Britain a year earlier. It was a vote for peace and order, for the firm execution of the Treaty of Versailles, for the repression of Bolshevism, and the defence of property and discipline and reconstruction at home. It looked as though France might have a period of strong and effective government.

Yet old traditions die hard and political ingratitude is notorious. Almost the first task of the new Chamber was to meet together with the Senate at Versailles as a National Assembly and elect a new President of the Republic. The obvious choice in the eyes of the world was Clemenceau. But Clemenceau hesitated to be a formal candidate although he allowed his sponsors to put his name forward. This weakened his position. He was authoritarian, Radical, and anti-clerical, while many in the new Chamber had Catholic sympathies. His enemies included powerful figures such as Poincaré, Foch, and the supple former Socialist Aristide Briand. The last two played on Catholic fears: for instance, Clemenceau might die in office and then the staunch old anti-clerical would have to have a state funeral without religious ceremonies. What a scandal that would be!

Thus Clemenceau's position was undermined by intriguers and in the first straw vote a rival candidate polled more votes. Clemenceau at once withdrew. The new President was Paul Deschanel, a relatively conservative politician whose main qualifications were his elegance and the tact with which he had presided over the Chamber. It was no new thing to turn a President of the Chamber into a President of the Republic, but, under the circumstances, it was as though in London the best-dressed Speaker of the House of Commons had been preferred to the greatest living Briton. The choice was doubly unfortunate. After nine months at the Elysée Deschanel had to be removed to a mental home.

Meanwhile, Clemenceau had resigned and retired into private life. He lived for ten more years and retained his mental powers almost to the end. The country was the

Right: *Union meeting at Vincennes protests against 'la vie chère'*

CONTRE LA VIE CHÈRE
C.G.T
DES METAUX
C.G.T

poorer for not having the sagacious leadership which he might yet have given it, even though the President lacked the power of a Prime Minister.

But the man Clemenceau would have made his Prime Minister had he become President was also Deschanel's choice. Alexandre Millerand, who had made history twenty-one years earlier as the first Socialist to enter a French cabinet, had moved well to the Right and had subsequently held many important posts. He had been chosen for the delicate task of High Commissioner in Alsace and Lorraine and he had helped to launch the *Bloc National* in which, after Clemenceau's retirement, he soon became the leading figure. Short and stocky, with bristly white hair and heavy black eyebrows and moustache, he was a man of few words who gave the impression of strength and determination. His cabinet was again a coalition in which, significantly, the Radicals, who had to be propitiated because of their influence in the Senate, contrived to secure the key post of the Ministry of the Interior. But it was also the government which stood firm against the wave of strikes in 1920 and which despatched General Weygand to Warsaw, thereby helping the Poles to repel the Bolshevik invasion which at one time looked like carrying all before it.

Millerand, however, did not remain Prime Minister for long. Although in November 1919 he had made clear his views that the constitution needed revising in order to strengthen the executive, when Deschanel resigned in September 1920 Millerand was the man whom the National Assembly elected in his place. Once at the Elysée, he showed that he did not intend to be a lame-duck. As a result, like MacMahon in 1877, he would eventually come into conflict with the legislature which, in 1919, he had accused of constantly 'usurping the attributions and rights of the executive power'.

With the signature of the Treaty of Versailles and its subsequent repudiation by the American Senate, the election of the *Chambre Bleu Horizon,* the retirement of Clemenceau, the choice of Millerand, the failure of the general strike, and the split in the Socialist Party, we come to the end of the period of transition from war to peace.

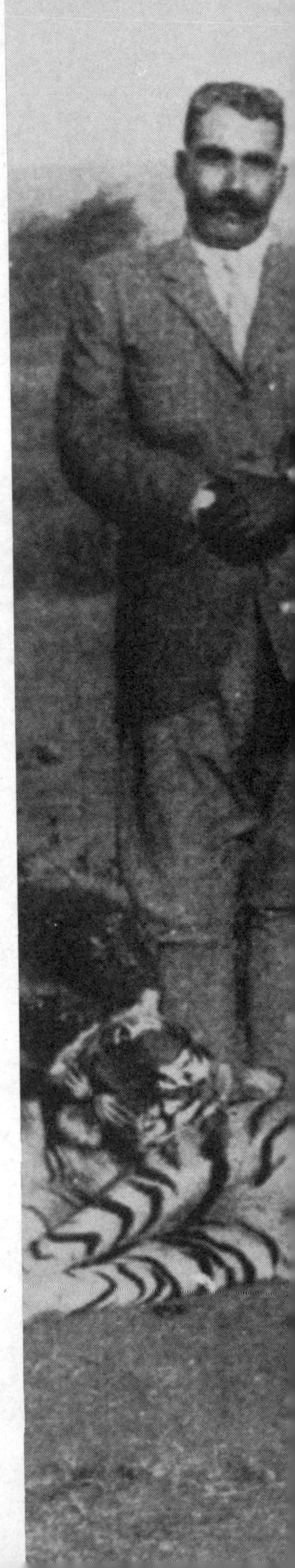

Right: *Clemenceau, the old 'tiger', on safari—his life work done*

Chapter 4

Reparations and the Ruhr

The Treaty of Versailles came into effect in January 1920. Soon after, one of France's best-known politicians, Briand, remarked, 'It is a faultless treaty. Like the legendary mare, it possesses every virtue but one: it hasn't the breath of life in it.' His words reflected France's growing anxiety at the policy of 'evasion, procrastination, and delay' (Lloyd George's words) which Germany pursued in meeting her obligations. This anxiety made French governments all the more disposed both to adopt a hard line towards Germany and to safeguard their country's security by a system of military alliances. Unfortunately both these objectives ran counter to British policies.

Clemenceau had been well aware that the continued friendship of the two great English-speaking nations was essential to France in the post-war era. It was largely for this reason that he made one journey abroad after his resignation and crossed the Atlantic in 1922 in an effort to restore good relations with the United States. But he was out of office, his voyage was criticised by enemies at home, and his influence was powerless to check America's isolationism or modify her critical attitude towards France.

With the prevailing American attitude set against active friendship with France, it was all the more important to maintain close harmony with Britain. But this too proved impossible. The British, at first no less hostile to Germany than the French, swung rapidly to a more lenient view of the supposedly democratic Weimar regime which had had to accept a dictated peace. Henceforward, British opinion was increasingly inclined to favour treaty revision, a scaling down of reparations, the economic rehabilitation of Germany, and her readmission to the comity of European nations on equal terms.

Co-operation continued for three years, but it was increasingly uneasy. Britain had rapidly demobilised and, apart from a garrison in her zone of occupation in the Rhineland, had pulled out her forces from the Continent.

Left: *The troops and armoured cars of the mightiest military power in Europe—en route to Essen on the Ruhr, 1923*

Much less powerful on land than France, she was all the more inclined to be jealous and to carp at developments in areas such as Upper Silesia where France was left with the main burden of keeping peace. The dead hand of the past still obscured men's views of the present. Thus in May 1920 a Foreign Office memorandum harked back to the quarrels of the 1890s and rejected the idea of building a Channel Tunnel because 'our relations [with France] never have been, are not, and probably never will be, sufficiently stable and friendly'; moreover, it complained, 'nothing could be more provocative than the attitude of the French press'. There was friction too over many other issues: the Near East for example, and over France's programme for building submarines, a type of war vessel which the British would have liked to ban altogether. Powerless to intervene effectively in Europe, British statesmen and publicists often succumbed to an old British temptation and addressed irresponsible homilies to their former ally.

The question of reparations

The greatest problem that bedevilled both Anglo-French relations and French finances during the years 1920-4 was reparation. The question would have been simplified had the treaty stated the total amount and fixed it in relation to Germany's capacity to pay. But it was claimed that the damages could not be assessed in time—to fix a definite figure so soon, said Lloyd George, was 'like asking a man in the maelstrom of Niagara to fix the price of a horse'—and it was left to a special Reparations Commission to determine the proper figure by 1st May 1921, and to draw up a scheme for payment of the whole debt over a period of thirty years. Meanwhile, at the Spa Conference in July 1920, agreement was reached on each country's share of the whole. The fact that France had been the largest sufferer was recognised: she was to receive fifty-two per cent, compared with twenty-two per cent for Britain and ten per cent for Italy. In consequence, it was natural that she should be the power most concerned to exact payment and to have the chief say in future decisions concerning reparation. But Millerand's request that priority of payment should be given to France as compensation for the damages in her

Right: *French cartoon of the republican legalist Poincaré. Inflexibly he demanded his pound of flesh: reparations were, for France, the keystone of Versailles.* ***Next page:*** *'The Rhine remains German!'—a protest at French aggression, 1923* ***(left)****; German hostility to the colonial troops of occupation is laid bare in this appeal 'To the conscience of the world' to take note of French 'atrocities'* ***(right)****.* ***Page 60:*** *Occupied Rhineland—a notice outside a French officers' club forbids entry to Germans*

DROITS
FEMME
CITOYENNE
DROITS
HOMME
CITOYE

Deutſch bleibt der Rhein!

1923

SIMPLICISSIMUS

Bezugspreis vierteljährlich 3000 Mark

Begründet von Albert Langen und Th. Th. Heine

Bezugspreis vierteljährlich 3000 Mark

An das Weltgewissen

(Karl Arnold)

Über das Märchen von den abgehackten Kinderhänden hat sich die ganze Welt entrüstet. Aber die Wahrheit findet taube Ohren.

Franzosisches
Offizier-Kasino
Eintritt
für Deutsche verboten

devastated areas was rejected by Lloyd George. Nevertheless, France went ahead with her reconstruction. She met the financial outlay not by reorganising her financial system and making income tax effective or by levying higher taxes, but by a continuation of the war-time policy of borrowing. The public were invited to subscribe to reconstruction loans and when war loans were redeemable they were replaced by new loans carrying still higher rates of interest. At the same time, alongside the normal budget, which continued to be balanced, a much larger 'extraordinary' or 'German' budget was instituted in the expectation that it would be covered by reparation payments received from Germany. Thus France's indebtedness grew, for she was already saddled with war debts. Consequently, she would not abate her claims on Germany below a sum adequate to meet both the charges of reconstruction and the amount of the war debts owed to former allies. When the United States in 1920 reaffirmed her refusal to cancel war debts, 'a fatal concatenation' began: 'The United States refused to forgo the debt due from Great Britain; thus burdened, Great Britain refused to forgo the debt due from France; denied relief in this direction, France refused to lighten the load on Germany.'

The reparation question highlights the core of the problem of transition from war to peace, in Germany no less than in France. Clemenceau had stressed the difficulty of winning the peace, but people were reluctant to face realities. They were in no mood for austerity, and the politicians were only too ready to humour them, since the issues of reparations and war debts created convenient scapegoats. Thus the German government continued the war-time policy of printing money rather than imposing an income tax, and spent four times its revenue in the first four years of its existence. At the same time Germany protested her inability to pay reparations. The French government set up the 'German budget' in similar circumstances, also shying away from handing on the burden to the taxpayer.

The three French Premiers who bore the main burden of putting France's reparations case after Millerand had become President of the Republic were Leygues, Briand, and Poincaré. But the Leygues ministry was short-lived, for he was regarded as a puppet of the President, and the Chamber, suspicious of any covert effort to increase the powers of the executive, soon brought about his downfall. His successor, Aristide Briand, was a man of greater calibre, who had already been six times Prime Minister. He was flexible and conciliatory, a man with an acute sense of political atmosphere and of what was possible, but his skill was to be tested to the utmost in the international conferences and negotiations during his year of office. He believed both in the importance of co-operation with Britain and in the value of diplomacy by conference. But when Germany looked like paying less and less in reparation, it was increasingly difficult to persuade a nationalist Chamber and a vociferous Right-wing press that conferences and negotiations did not merely result in further concessions by France. The question of applying sanctions, if Germany continued to default, loomed larger as time went on, and sanctions meant above all the occupation of the great industrial area of the Ruhr on the east bank of the Rhine.

The question of sanctions had already come up as early as April 1920. Eleven months later, when Germany was still in default and made an offer of reparation payment that was regarded as derisory, Allied troops had by way of sanctions occupied three towns on the right bank of the Rhine: Düsseldorf, Ruhrort, and Duisburg. Then, when Germany's attitude still appeared obstructive, she had been given an ultimatum threatening occupation of the Ruhr if she did not accept an agreed schedule of reparations and fulfil certain other obligations relating to disarmament and war criminals. The ultimatum was accepted by a new German government and for a time there was something of a détente.

Meanwhile, Germany's economic difficulties were increasing with growing inflation and in December 1921 she asked for a moratorium on reparation payments. Lloyd George feared that economic collapse in Germany would be followed by Bolshevik revolutions in Central Europe. In consequence, at the next conference, held at Cannes in January 1922, he made a dramatic attempt to induce Briand to modify France's intransigent attitude and to reduce Anglo-French tension. In return for French co-operation in European reconstruction, an economic arrangement with Soviet Russia, the cessation of naval rivalry, and the co-ordination of French and British policies in the Near East, he offered to revive the British guarantee to come to France's aid should she be attacked by Germany. But France wanted both reparation and security, if possible on her own terms. The French cabinet profoundly disliked the idea of any dealings with Russia and they wanted not a unilateral guarantee from Britain but an alliance of which, in Millerand's words, the basis would be 'absolute equality between the two contracting parties', and the object 'the integral execution of the treaties'. Briand was quickly made aware that the British proposals were unpalatable in their existing form, and a suspicious Senate and Chamber, reinforced by a

***Right:** Briand (on right) is taught golf by Lloyd George, 1922. Frenchmen feared that the lesson extended to politics as well*

FRENCH MILITARISM
ALLIANCE
THE NEXT WAR

hostile press which published sensational reports of a Franco-British alliance in which France was the subordinate partner, soon made his position untenable. The last straw, perhaps, was the report that Lloyd George had been teaching him to play golf. What better proof that he had been diddled by the British Prime Minister who must have had him in his pocket? He promptly returned to Paris, was greeted with jeers by a crowd mobilised by the *Action Française,* and adroitly resigned before a vote was taken. The Cannes Conference came to a premature end, French nationalism had asserted itself more vigorously than ever, and the gulf between France and Britain had been widened. Briand's day was temporarily done, Poincaré's was at hand.

Millerand took an unprecedented step when he invited Poincaré to be Briand's successor. No former President of the Republic had been called upon subsequently to take cabinet office. But the circumstances were exceptional and Poincaré the nationalist was attuned to the prevailing mood. There could have been no greater contrast than that between Poincaré and Briand, the most flexible and charming of politicians, who had friends and contacts in all camps. Poincaré was a man who had a justified reputation for personal integrity and financial expertise. At the same time he was a dedicated patriot who cordially detested the Germans. Briand, indolent, devious, and conciliatory, had the wider vision, whereas Poincaré, a lawyer by training, was hard-working, rigid, intransigent, and unimaginative; someone said of them: 'Briand knows nothing and understands everything; Poincaré knows everything and understands nothing.' Poincaré's nomination meant that French policy towards Germany would be still more unyielding.

The negotiations and arrangements made at Cannes were not all broken but thenceforth had to continue in a chillier climate. Poincaré, like most French statesmen, recognised the value of a British alliance but, like Millerand, he and his colleagues wanted both an alliance of equal partners and one that would cover not merely France's frontier but the demilitarised zone and eastern Europe. It would be many years before Britain would contemplate such wide commitments. Meanwhile, the other chief consequence of Cannes was a meeting at Genoa in April at which all the main powers, including Soviet Russia, were represented. It achieved little beyond

Top left: *German cartoons fear that Poincaré's belligerence has spread to England* ***(left)*** *and show a gluttonous French general, flanked by a Senegalese soldier, dining sumptuously while the Ruhr starves* ***(right). Bottom:*** *'Love me—love my dog!'— Low's comment on Anglo-French understanding* revealing once more the sharp antagonism between France and Russia. But it had an important subsidiary result. The Germans seized the opportunity to arrange a separate meeting with the Russians at nearby Rapallo. There they signed an agreement to re-establish diplomatic relations, liquidate financial claims, and explore economic co-operation. The news of this rapprochement came like a bolt from the blue to the other powers. Its effect was to intensify suspicions of Germany, particularly in France. In the following month it seemed to a well-known Left-wing English visitor to France, H.J.Laski, that Frenchmen already feared a new war. They still regarded Germany, he said, as 'the origin of all wrong and suffering, prosperous in fact, and falsely declaring herself bankrupt to win the pity of soft-hearted England. Yet not entirely soft-hearted. For, having destroyed the German fleet, England has no menace to confront. . . . The foreigner cannot measure the sacrifice France has made. . . . If there is disharmony in Europe it is because Versailles has not been enforced.'

By the end of the year Anglo-French relations had further worsened because of a rift over Near Eastern affairs. In the summer of 1922 the Nationalist Turks launched a successful offensive against a Greek army which was occupying Western Turkey. The Turks threatened to press their attack into Eastern Europe, and Lloyd George wished to place an international army at the Dardanelles to oppose their invasion. But Poincaré ordered the withdrawal of the French contingent. There was an acrimonious exchange between him and Lord Curzon, the British Foreign Secretary, who was furious at being worsted by 'that horrid little man'.

Soon afterwards Lloyd George fell from power and his Conservative successor, Bonar Law, was less disposed to play a flamboyant part in Continental affairs. Meanwhile, Germany's economic difficulties persisted and the mark continued to fall. At the end of 1922 she asked for a further moratorium for three or four years as a necessary preliminary to the stabilisation of her currency and for the fixing of her liabilities at a sum 'which could be defrayed from the budget surplus'. By then Poincaré's patience was exhausted. He regarded this request as further proof of Germany's bad faith. The time had come to enforce the treaty and carry out the long threatened occupation of the Ruhr. His policy was backed by the great majority in the Chamber apart from the Communists, Socialists, and some prudent Radicals. On 11th January 1923 French and Belgian troops moved across the Rhine. But they were not supported by any British contingents.

***Right:** French West African troops in the Rhineland, 1923*

The British government thoroughly disapproved of the occupation and maintained an attitude of frigid neutrality. The gulf between the former Allies had, as Bonar Law said, become too wide for any bridge to span.

Invasion, resistance, withdrawal

The immediate aim of the French and Belgians was to enforce the payment of reparations by securing 'productive pledges' and taking control of the great industries in the Ruhr. The sanctions were economic and the soldiers were there to protect the special mission whose task it was to collect reparations. The ultimate aim was to force the German government to modify its whole attitude to the reparation question. But the Germans were infuriated and resorted to passive resistance. The government encouraged the Ruhr workers to go on strike, acts of sabotage were committed, and officials refused to help the occupying powers. The French and German press indulged in a veritable cold war of abuse. But passive resistance was by no means total. The French set up a customs barrier separating the occupied area from the rest of Germany. French and Belgian technicians were brought in to operate the mines and railways, and separatist movements were, not very successfully, encouraged. In these circumstances, the Ruhr coal owners, increasingly hard hit, opposed the demand for a general strike and permitted the mines to be worked and coal deliveries to be collected by the French.

For Germany the cost of passive resistance was ruinous. It gave the final impetus to still greater inflation and a consequent collapse of the currency. It also precipitated a fresh government crisis and in September 1923 a new cabinet, headed by Gustav Stresemann, formally abandoned passive resistance and agreed to resume reparation payments. France's determination seemed to have triumphed. But her victory was only partial. She had forced Germany to her knees, but Poincaré had not the imagination to follow up his victory with any dramatic gesture. In the eyes of many Frenchmen, including Foch and Millerand, he missed the greatest opportunity that occurred between the wars of negotiating a direct agreement with Germany from a position of strength. Such a negotiation would have been logical in view of the critical or hostile attitude of many of France's former allies, but whether Poincaré would have got the better of the wily Stresemann is debatable. Instead, however, sensitive at last to France's increasing isolation and yielding to

Right: *The Franco-Belgian occupation of the Ruhr, beyond France's eastern frontier. The enterprise finally backfired*

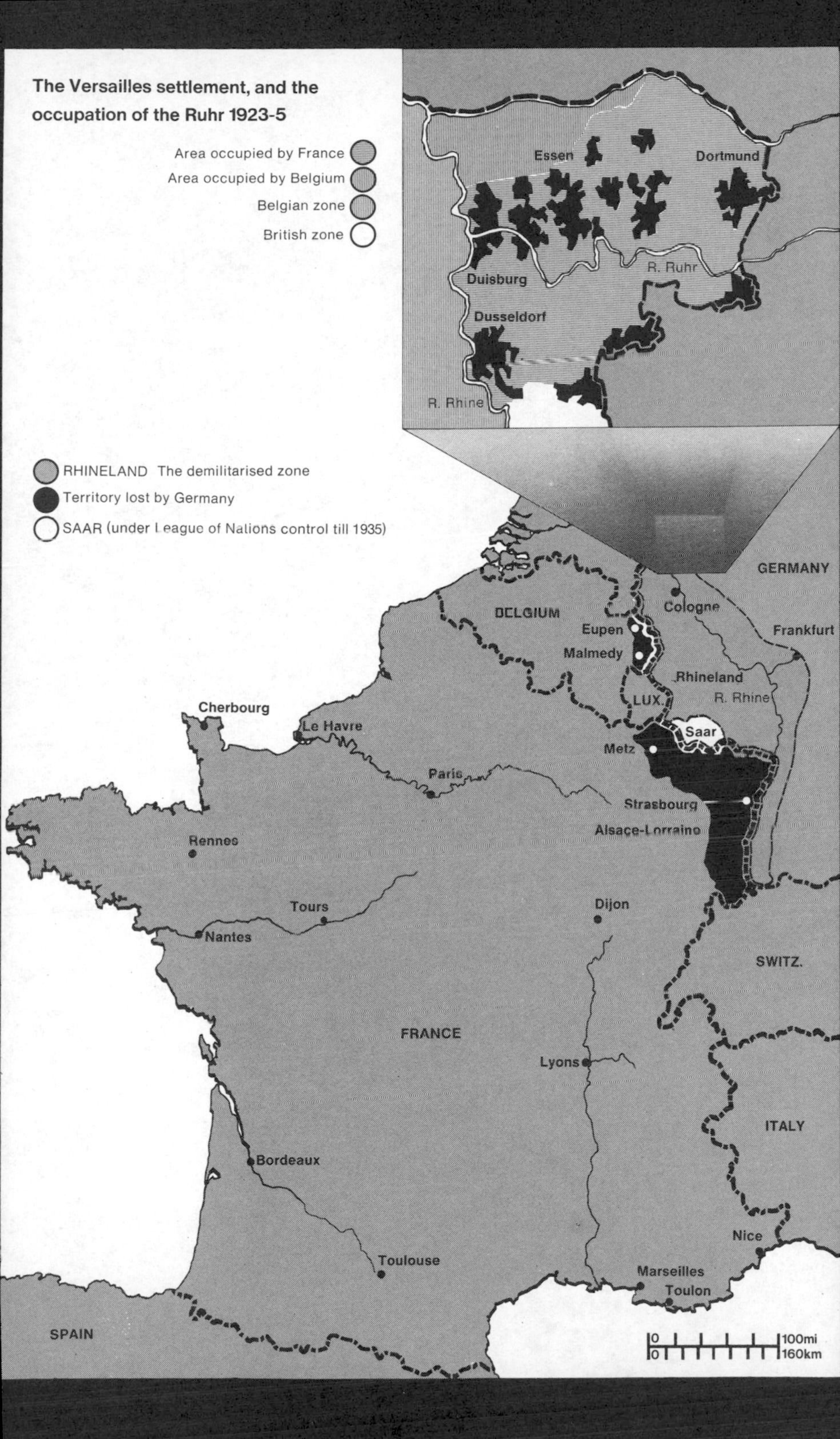

The Versailles settlement, and the occupation of the Ruhr 1923-5
Area occupied by France
Area occupied by Belgium
Belgian zone
British zone
Essen
Dortmund
R. Ruhr
Duisburg
Dusseldorf
R. Rhine
RHINELAND The demilitarised zone
Territory lost by Germany
SAAR (under League of Nations control till 1935)
GERMANY
BELGIUM
Cologne
Eupen
Malmedy
Frankfurt
Rhineland
R. Rhine
LUX.
Saar
Metz
Cherbourg
Le Havre
Paris
Strasbourg
Alsace-Lorraine
Rennes
Tours
Nantes
Dijon
SWITZ.
FRANCE
Lyons
ITALY
Bordeaux
Nice
Toulouse
Marseilles
Toulon
SPAIN
0 100mi
0 160km

strong American pressure, he agreed to a suggestion that the twin problems of reparations and the stabilisation of the mark should be referred to two expert committees. To his nationalist critics at home he seemed unexpectedly timorous: he was, they said, only a lath painted to look like iron.

By April 1924 the new reparation committee headed by the American General Charles G.Dawes had devised a reparation plan which would before long be accepted by all parties. But by then Poincaré's position at home was being undermined. Economically the Ruhr occupation was proving a calamity for France as well as for Germany. The amounts collected in reparation were relatively small and the costs of occupation were considerable. Consequently French indebtedness increased, prices continued to rise, and the franc itself showed signs of strain. People began to fear that it might go the way of the mark and that they would be ruined. Thus the result of the occupation was not more reparation, but what the French public and politicians had alike sought to avoid, more taxation. The Ruhr policy rapidly lost popularity and its Left-wing critics, reinforced by a vigorous new Paris paper *Le Quotidien,* were increasingly vocal. Poincaré was no longer extolled as the man who would make Germany pay. He became *'Poincaré la guerre', 'Poincaruhr',* the man whose belligerent obstinacy might lead France into war and had led to the weakness of the franc. Many Radicals, those prudent weathercocks, hesitated to support Poincaré's policies. By now they had left the *Bloc National* and renewed friendship with the Socialists. Poincaré remade his cabinet in March but this did not mend matters. 'Long live the spring,' exclaimed the *Quotidien.* 'An end to heating, lighting, and the *Bloc National.'*

So it was. Poincaré was neither by standing nor temperament the man to lead a rousing election campaign. When the allotted span of the *Chambre Bleu Horizon* expired and fresh elections were held in May 1924 there was a swing to the Left. Poincaré and his policies were rejected and a Left-wing coalition, known as the *Cartel des Gauches,* emerged as the victor. One of its first acts was to arrange to end the Ruhr occupation and to accept the Dawes Plan. France's relations with Britain and Germany would now enter a new phase, the reparation problem would become less acute, and new means would be sought to meet the still unresolved problem of French security.

Left: *The reparations committee, headed by American general Dawes and financier Young (centre), meets in Paris in 1923 to plan the compromise that will end the unfortunate Ruhr affair*

Chapter 5

The *Cartel* in Power

Significant for their effect upon French foreign policy, the elections of 1924 were also significant at home. They marked a reversion to the more normal political pattern in which the country was governed by a coalition of anticlerical Centre and Left-wing groups instead of the Right. But the *Cartel's* victory was far less resounding than that of the Bloc National in 1919 and so, when it met with difficulties, there was a new period of ministerial instability. The very name *Cartel,* first used in Germany at the end of the 19th century to denote a political grouping, meant a combination of groups associated to advance their own interests. Such a combination could hold together only so long as the groups concerned could agree on their main political aims. Its durability would depend upon its ability to cope with the economic and financial problems which had baffled its predecessors and which baffled most European statesmen of the inter-war period. Meanwhile, it brought to the fore a number of men who would be leading political figures during the ensuing decade. It also precipitated a Presidential crisis.

The victory of the *Cartel* was to a considerable extent brought about by the small man, scared by the prospect of higher taxes, monetary collapse, and financial ruin. The Radical leader Edouard Herriot had said that the *Cartel* was fighting against 'the new feudalism of economic powers' and for fiscal equality. It wanted to lower the cost of living, introduce social reforms, and maintain the secular state. Such a programme naturally appealed to those living on pensions or fixed incomes, to the working man, to the numerous subordinate civil servants throughout the country who feared the economic axe, and also to the 'lay' committees and state school teachers who mistrusted reconciliation with the Church. These were the people who had voted for the Left, above all for the Socialists and Radicals – the Socialists now finding their main strength in towns which had been Radical strongholds, while the Radicals appealed to the small men in

Left: *Edouard Herriot, well-meaning leader of the Radical Party and the epitome of the provincial French politician*

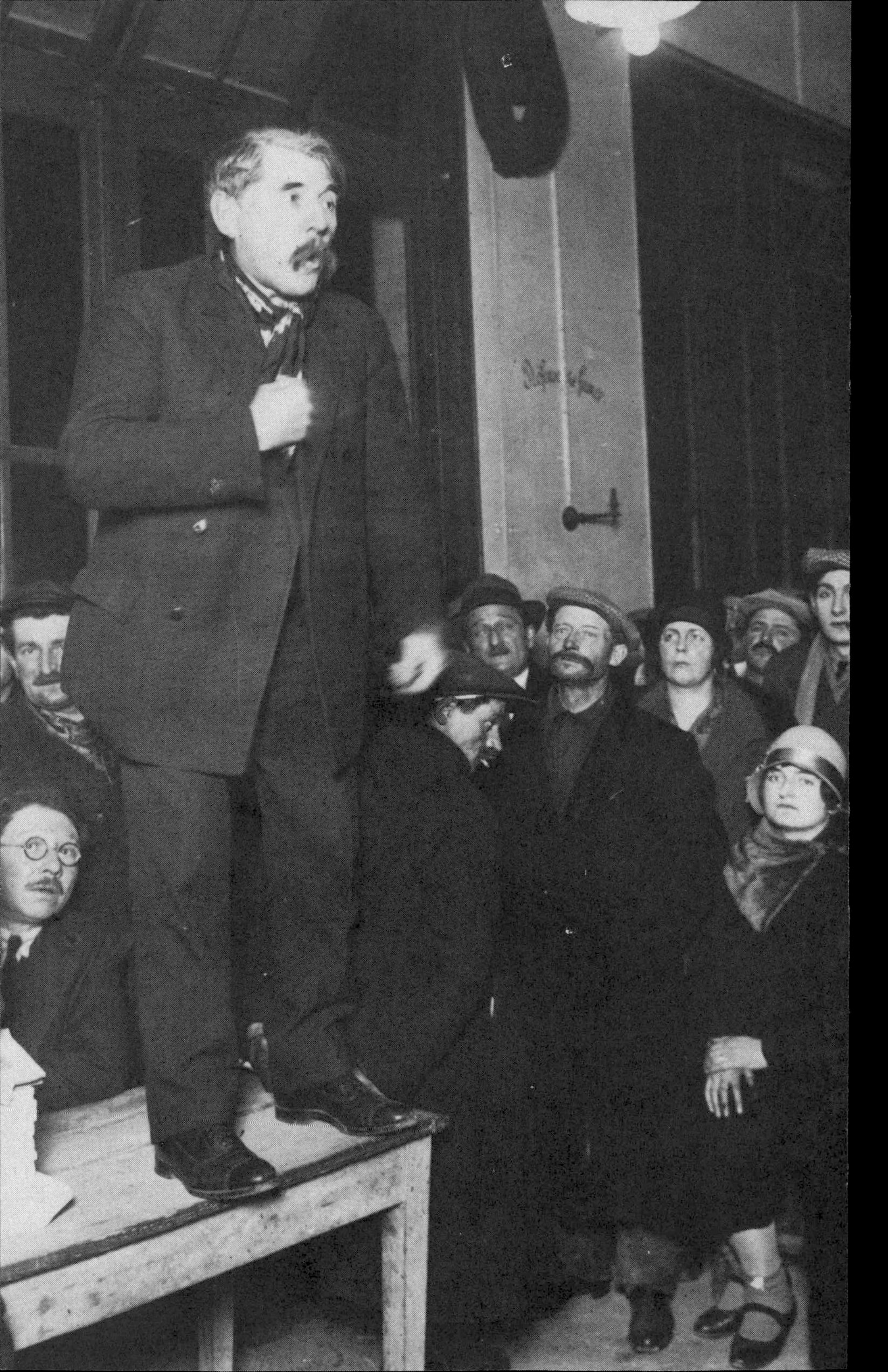

the provinces, particularly in the south. Although the Communists had carried away the majority when the Socialists split in 1920, the remaining Socialists under the able leadership of Léon Blum and Paul Faure had been remarkably successful in rebuilding their party's fortunes. The willowy Jewish intellectual Blum, with the aid of Jewish financiers, had founded a newspaper, *Le Populaire,* and it replaced the now Communist *L'Humanité.* It had an uphill struggle to establish itself, but this did not impede the electoral success of the party, which in 1924 won 101 seats compared with some 130 gained by the Radicals. The fortunes of the Communists, on the other hand, after the euphoria of their first months as a separate party, had sharply declined. The Soviet honeymoon was brief. Party members soon found themselves ruthlessly dictated to and regimented by Moscow. The result was that most of those with any independence of mind either deserted or were purged. By the end of 1923 membership had dropped from 130,000 to 45,000. In 1924 the Socialists understandably refused a Communist invitation to join in 'a great workers' party'. They knew that the Communists' object was, as one of them said, 'to pluck the Socialist fowl'. The Communist Party therefore played a solitary hand and won only twenty-six seats. At daggers drawn with the Socialist Party, the *frère ennemi* from whom it had separated, it was the lone and hungry wolf of the Left, a kind of parliamentary pariah. But it was not, as some people thought, on the point of expiry. Moscow knew what it was doing.

One point on which the parliamentary groups of the *Cartel* were agreed from the outset was hostility to Millerand, the President of the Republic. The Socialists disliked him as a pre-war deserter from their ranks, while the Left in general mistrusted a man who wanted to revise the constitution and strengthen the executive. Moreover, he was accused of having transgressed the limits of his office in making a speech at Evreux in October 1923 which was not just a string of Presidential banalities, but in which, according to *Le Temps,* he exercised his right to talk politics to the nation. He did so largely because of Poincaré's reluctance to defend the record of the *Bloc National* and outline a clear programme in view of the forthcoming elections. But what he said was more like the speech of a Prime Minister than a President. In the circumstances it was a blunder and the men of the *Cartel* were eager for his blood. One of their papers, *Le Quotidien,* declared that they must have 'all the places and at once' and this included the Presidency. When,

***Left:** Marcel Cachin, a founder of the Moscow-controlled French Communist Party, addresses a meeting of the faithful*

after the elections, Poincaré resigned without meeting the new parliament, Millerand could find no one in the new majority willing to form a cabinet; the situation resembled that which had confronted a former President in 1887 – the potential Prime Ministers went on strike. Faced by this reluctance, he sought to justify his position and secure backing for a minority cabinet by addressing a message to the two Chambers. Had the Senate given him a vote of confidence, he might have been strong enough to win its consent to dissolve the Chamber. But the upper house rejected the policy of the message by ten votes. He had no choice but to resign.

The Senate's failure to support Millerand had been a crucial factor in his overthrow. Its influence was also demonstrated in the ensuing Presidential election. Almost every President of the Senate since 1899 had stood for the Presidency and now the two chief candidates were Paul Painlevé, the President of the Chamber, who was supported by the Left wing of the *Cartel,* and the more conservative Gaston Doumergue, President of the Senate. Doumergue was chosen by a large majority and his election was in a sense a first rebuff for the *Cartel.* He was a politician of the traditional type. When Millerand on the eve of his election as President of the Republic in 1920 had declared that although he did not intend to be a party man he had a decided policy which he hoped to carry out in collaboration with his ministers, Doumergue had at once reacted. In his view, the President's prerogatives were adequate, it would be 'extremely dangerous to make an innovation and give the President of the Republic *carte blanche* to execute a programme'. He had persuaded his group, the Democratic Left, to support a motion repudiating 'a policy which would tend to substitute the power of the Elysée for that of parliament and the country'. 'Gastounet', as the song-writers called him, the President with the amiable, fatherly smile, was evidently a safe man.

Cartel – the strange hybrid

Once the presidential crisis was over, a cabinet was formed by the Radical Edouard Herriot. But its composition immediately demonstrated one of the weaknesses of the *Cartel*: it contained no Socialists. The Socialists had always been troubled about participating in a 'bourgeois' government and their leader, Léon Blum, was at all costs eager to preserve the party's independence. He had found an ingenious way out of its dilemma by enunciating the theory that the party could only properly 'exercise power' when it was itself the largest party in a coalition. In 1924 the Radicals were the largest party in the *Cartel* and accordingly the Socialists refused

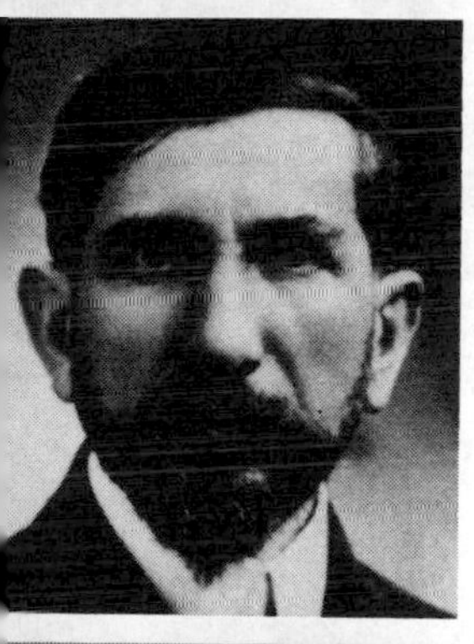

to participate in the government but promised it their 'loyal support' in parliament. It was a difficult kind of partnership to sustain, since it meant that, apart from ordinary cabinets, Herriot and his colleagues had to hold special meetings with the Socialist leaders in order to reach agreement on political objectives, strategy, and tactics. These meetings were frequently prolonged far into the night.

The Left had often had more pretentions to intellectual distinction than the Right and the new ministry and its chief supporters seemed particularly to exemplify this trait. Herriot himself, Léon Blum, and the mathematician Paul Painlevé, who now became a leading minister and was almost continuously in office between 1925 and 1933, were all three brilliant products of the École Normale, while a newcomer, Edouard Daladier, a baker's son, of whom more would be heard, had at one time taught in a Lycée. The academic or intellectual background of many of those now to the fore was conspicuous enough for one talented essayist to dub the new era 'the Republic of the Professors' – those who later in another country would rudely be called the 'egg-' or 'pointy-' heads were in control. But this did not mean that government would be wiser or more competent. Widely cultivated though many of them were, the new men were professional politicians like their predecessors. Herriot had been the very efficient mayor of France's second city, Lyons, since 1905, and had become France's youngest senator in 1912. With his pipe and his air of rugged simplicity he was in some ways the counterpart of the English Conservative leader, Baldwin, who had succeeded Bonar Law as Prime Minister but had been defeated in the election of December 1923. A talented orator, with interests which ranged from Beethoven and Mme de Récamier to gastronomy, Herriot was none the less bound to the existing political system of which his party had so often been the beneficiary. If the system needed modifying, he would hardly be the man to reform it. Indeed the inclusion of *'laicité'* or an anti-clerical policy as a main plank in the *Cartel's* programme showed how much some of its leaders, particularly the Radicals, were obsessed by the past.

The war, which had rallied Frenchmen of all creeds

Left: *Political personalities of the period –* ***(left-hand column from top)*** *Millerand, ex-Socialist leader of the Bloc National; his successor as President, the 'safe' Doumergue; Painlevé, several times Premier; Briand, Foreign Minister 1926-32.* ***Right-hand column:*** *Thorez, young leader of the Communists; General de Castelnau, Catholic monarchist; Maurras, founder of Action Française; Léon Daudet, Right-wing polemicist*

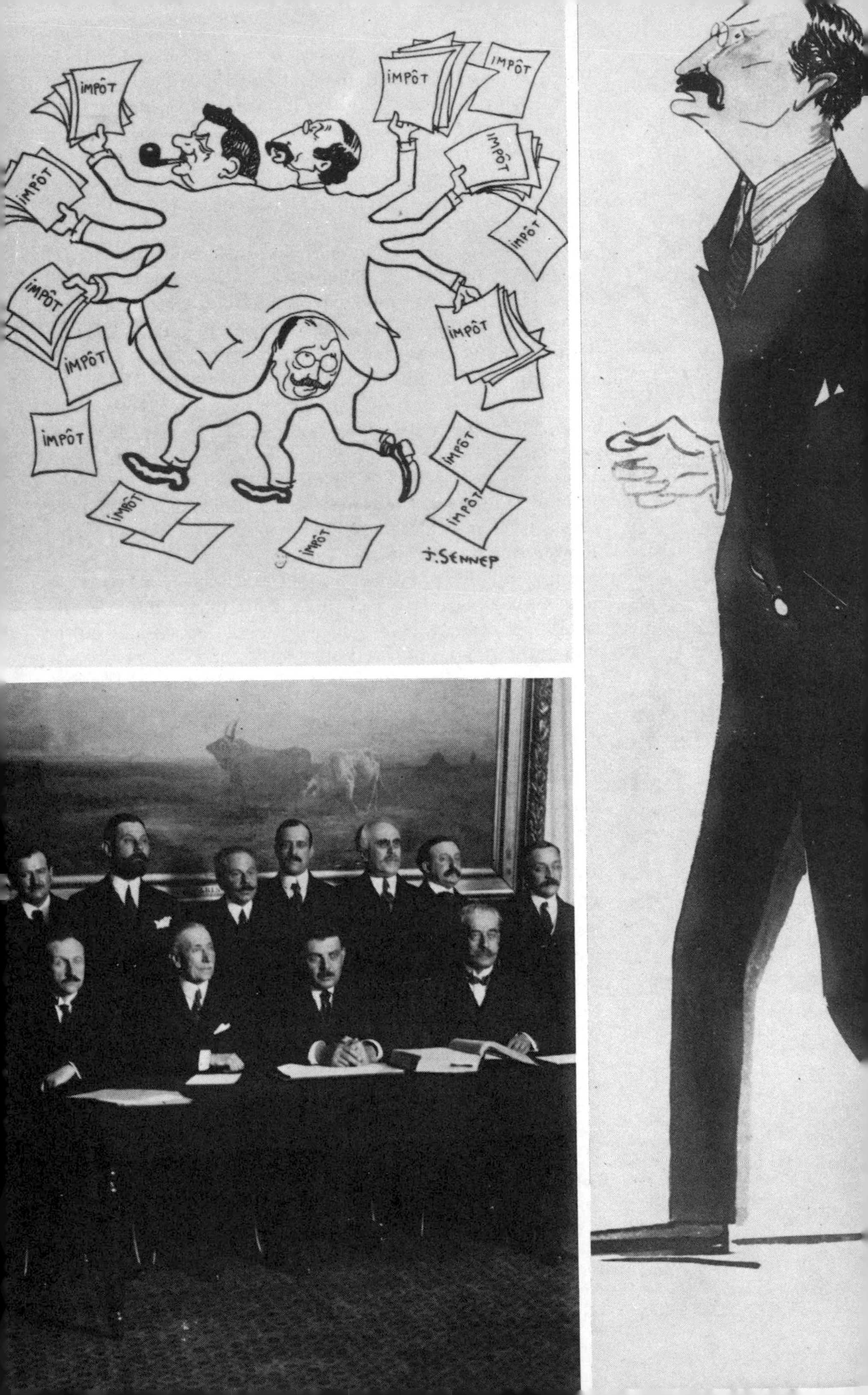
IMPÔT
IMPÔT
IMPÔT
IMPÔT
IMPÔT
IMPÔT
IMPÔT
IMPÔT
IMPÔT
IMPÔT
IMPÔT
IMPÔT
IMPÔT
IMPÔT
J. SENNEP

LÉON
BLUM

BIB

to defend their country, and the comradeship in the trenches of priest and layman, Catholic and unbeliever, had done much to allay the old hatreds of clerical and anti-clerical that had earlier loomed so large. The victory of the *Bloc National* had reinforced the trend towards reconciliation. Many religious teaching orders were allowed to work again in France. Catholics even vainly hoped that parliament might subsidise private schools by agreeing to '*répartition proportionnelle scolaire*', or the division of public funds between state and private schools in proportion to the number of pupils in each. The government was officially represented at the canonisation of Joan of Arc in Rome in 1920 and the cult of St Joan provided a new focus for Catholic ardour and Right-wing demonstrations. A year later diplomatic relations with the Papacy, severed since the separation of Church and State in 1905, were restored, and soon there was once again a French Embassy to the Vatican.

But all these developments were looked at with increasing dislike by the anti-clericals of the *Cartel*. It was clear that they would launch a counter-offensive once they were in power. It was relatively simple to reply to the canonisation of Joan of Arc by transferring the remains of the great pre-war Socialist leader Jean Jaurès to the Panthéon, the national shrine in Paris in which many of France's great men repose; but that part of the programme affecting the living rather than the dead was not so easy to implement without political and financial embarrassment. Thus Radicals and Socialists had both included educational reform in their election manifestos. What they particularly wanted was 'equality of all children with regard to instruction'. In other words, they demanded '*l'école unique*' or a single primary school instead of the existing system in which elementary instruction was given both in the free state primary schools and in the lower forms of the separately organised state secondary schools or *lycées*, where tuition and other charges were imposed. But this demand would necessitate a costly and drastic change in the educational structure. Although he had been from the outset one of its chief protagonists, Herriot, in his ministerial declaration in June 1924, alluded to the *école unique* only in the most general terms when he said that French democracy would not be safe 'so long as access to secondary education is determined by the wealth of the parents and not . . . by the merit of the children'. But he had stated that the Vatican Embassy would be withdrawn, that the laws against religious teaching orders would be en-

Far left: *The many-headed Cartel of 1924—as seen by Sennep* ***(top)*** *and in practice* ***(bottom).*** ***Left:*** *Socialist leader Léon Blum*

forced, and that the government would hasten the advent of the day when the last legislative difference will be effaced between the recovered departments [in Alsace and Lorraine] and the whole of the territory of the republic'. In so doing he roused old antagonisms and created new ones especially among those whom he had called the 'dear peoples finally restored to France'.

The two provinces of Alsace and Lorraine had led lives separate from France since 1870, and had known nothing of French republican anti-clericalism of the late 19th century. Alsace in particular was in a special position. She was a stronghold of ardent Catholicism, and three-quarters of her population were Catholics. Priests and pastors were still paid by the state, primary schools were run by the clergy, and religious instruction was compulsory in secondary schools. The obverse of the separation of church and state in France had been the struggle of the Alsatians to preserve their identity against Germany, and the leaders of this struggle for autonomy had been the priests. France had made war-time promises that in the event of victory she would maintain the religious and cultural rights of the Alsatians and hitherto the government had honoured these promises. A special High Commission to administer Alsace had been set up in Strasbourg and Alsatian susceptibilities had been scrupulously respected. Now the *Cartel* wanted both to impose unwanted centralisation, transferring the responsibility for administration to an office in Paris, and also to introduce the whole of republican legislation to the recovered provinces. This meant the separation of church and state and menaced church schools. The Catholic majority of the population was up in arms. The *Cartel's* ill-advised policy gave a powerful impetus to a new autonomist movement, in which priests who had been trained in Germany and regarded the lay state as an abomination were prominent leaders.

This Catholic resistance to the government's policies soon spread to the rest of France where it found a vigorous champion in General de Castelnau, famous as one of the defenders of Verdun. He and his friends formed a National Catholic Federation and, Sunday after Sunday in the autumn and winter of 1924-5, they arranged mass demonstrations of protest against the government's religious policies. In March 1925 the whole French hierarchy joined in the controversy with a violent condemnation of the government's proposals. Thanks largely to 'the booted Capuchin', as his enemies called Castelnau, the Catholics had for the first time successfully organised on a national

Left: *The* Camelots du Roi *attempt a demonstration on the fête-day of Joan of Arc, adopted symbol of the Right, Paris 1925*

scale in defence of their religious interests. In 1925 Herriot's successor, Painlevé, quietly ended the anticlerical offensive and even appointed a champion of the Vatican Embassy as Minister of Education. The embassy was maintained, the religious orders were not proceeded against, and republican legislation was not after all introduced into Alsace. As for the *école unique,* by the end of 1925 the Minister for Education had to admit that it was but a generous dream. But much damage had been done and the autonomist movement continued to exist, although by no means commanding the support of all Alsatian Catholics.

Collapse of the *Cartel*

Inheritor of a serious financial situation, Herriot's cabinet started off on a wrong footing. It needed to restore nation-wide confidence, but its allies on the Left soon talked of measures highly alarming to conservatives and to orthodox financial interests. The CGT and the Socialists wanted to reduce interest rates on government bonds. They also demanded a capital levy, and one prominent Socialist declared that 'they would take the money where it was to be found'. The cry 'the Germans will pay' had given way to 'the rich will pay'. Confidence was further impaired and when several short-term Treasury bonds were due for redemption many investors, including several who had voted for the *Cartel,* demanded repayment. The application of the Dawes Plan and the resumption of German reparation payments only temporarily arrested a further fall of the franc. Faced by demands for repayment, the Treasury had to appeal to the Bank of France to increase its note circulation. But this had a statutory limit or ceiling of 41 milliard francs and still more was needed. When it was discovered in April 1925 that the ceiling had been exceeded by two milliards there was an outcry and a fresh crisis. The worsening situation had already led to the resignation of the Finance Minister and Herriot's majority in the Chamber had dropped by nearly forty votes. Now the Senate refused a vote of confidence and the cabinet fell. Herriot had found himself up against what, in a famous phrase, he denounced as the '*mur d'argent*' (wall of capital) presented by the orthodox banking and financial interests who had refused to support him. But the Right claimed that this refusal was not the result of any deliberate attempt to sabotage a Left-wing administration, but simply the natural reaction to unsound policies. **86** ▷

***Right:** Léon Daudet, having barricaded himself in the* Action Française *newspaper offices to avoid arrest, is called upon by Jean Chiappe, prefect of the Paris police, to surrender, 1927*

L'ACTION FRAN

Revolt in Morocco

France's overseas empire included Indo-China and vast tracts of West Africa, and was peopled, in the words of a government memorandum, 'by 60 million inhabitants. It covered an area equal to twenty-three times that of the home country'. In 1925 an incident occurred which in some respects foreshadowed later anti-colonial liberation movements. In 1921 Abd-el-Krim (seen **right** with fellow warriors and next to a European journalist) had annihilated a Spanish army in Spanish Morocco and was soon to proclaim a republic. In 1925 he attacked a tribe from the neighbouring protectorate of French Morocco. In the ensuing struggle the armies of Generals Navarro (1) and Berenguer (2) **(below right)** proved too strong—but not before Abd-el-Krim, a traditional tribal leader, had evoked the sympathies of the French Communist Party and the German people **(below:** a German cartoon shows Abd-el-Krim shielding Morocco from the jackals and vultures of French imperialism)

1
2

In any case, Herriot's resignation was the beginning of the end of the *Cartel*.

Herriot's successor, Painlevé, called upon Joseph Caillaux, the one man on the Left who still had a reputation as a financial wizard, to assume the now thankless post of Minister of Finance. Caillaux had fallen into disgrace during the war and been arrested in 1918. His return to office was something of a sensation, but the Left were glad to recall a man whom they regarded as a martyr to Clemenceau's vindictiveness. Yet in matters of finance he was no Socialist and his orthodox proposals, including one for a loan on flexible terms which should have attracted far-sighted investors, were unavailing. In October Painlevé resigned in turn and, during the following nine months, there was a veritable 'cascade' of falling cabinets and 'expert' finance ministers. These *Cartel* governments could follow no coherent policy but oscillated between the extreme proposals dear to the Socialists and the more conservative plans preferred by the Radicals. Ministerial instability was at its height. Painlevé succeeded Painlevé, Briand, formerly anathema to the *Cartel* because of his association with the *Bloc National*, was recalled and headed three (his eighth, ninth, and tenth) cabinets in succession, but he, too, was unsuccessful. In June 1925, as a last resort, Caillaux was called in again. By then the franc had fallen to 174 to the pound. The situation seemed so critical that Caillaux made an unprecedented demand. He asked for full powers to carry out by decree the recommendations of a committee of experts set up by his predecessor. But Caillaux had a past which, a member of the Right declared, had 'the inconvenience of dividing Frenchmen and that is a serious consideration when one is trying to restore confidence'. Moreover, the grant of special powers ran counter to Radical principles, since it would weaken the deputies' direct control. Herriot, now President of the Chamber, rose in wrath and descended into the arena to denounce the proposal. It was the stab in the back which finally killed the *Cartel*. When, on 18th July 1926, the man who had delivered the stab was called on in turn to save the situation, he lasted only forty-eight hours.

Right: *French rule over Syria and Lebanon is established by the proclamation of a League of Nations mandate in Beirut, 1920*

Chapter 6

The Search for Security

Deprived of the Anglo-American guarantees on which Clemenceau had pinned his faith, and dubious of the power of President Wilson's brain-child, the infant League of Nations, to hold out a protective shield, French statesmen in 1919 and after looked elsewhere for support. The result was the gradual construction of a system of alliances intended to maintain the status quo of the treaty settlements, and to be a reinsurance against aggression by the former enemy. The first of these alliances was concluded with a neighbour who was no less preoccupied with security. The German invasion of Belgium in 1914 had shown the hollowness of any guarantee of Belgian neutrality, and the Belgian government would have liked to conclude a tripartite alliance with France and Britain. But Britain refused to undertake new commitments, whereas France, whose flank had been exposed by the German invasion, was eager to do so and ready to make concessions to obtain Belgium's alliance. Franco-Belgian negotiations went ahead and a military agreement for a co-ordinated system of defence of the two countries' frontiers with Germany was signed in Paris on 30th July 1920 by Marshal Foch and the Belgian General Maglinse. It was as a natural consequence of this agreement that Belgium had participated in the occupation of the Ruhr.

But France had also traditionally looked for allies in Eastern Europe. In 1920 France, as we have seen, had been Poland's champion against Soviet invasion and the conclusion of an alliance was the natural sequel to this chivalrous revival of an ancient friendship between two of the leading Catholic nations of East and West. In February 1921 the masterful Polish head of state, Marshal Piłsudski, visited Paris and a treaty was signed together with

Left: *The signatories of Locarno gather outside 11 Downing Street, London, official residence of the Chancellor of the Exchequer Winston Churchill (leaning on railings), December 1925. Front row from left: Vandervelde (Belgium), Briand, Luther (Germany), Baldwin. Austen Chamberlain is at the back (with monocle), Stresemann (bald-headed) behind* a military convention providing for mutual assistance in case of unprovoked attack by a third power.

But this was not enough. South of the Carpathians and around the Danube basin there lay the five succession states of the former Habsburg Empire. Here too French diplomacy had been active, seeking to substitute French influence for that of Germany which had predominated before the war. France had helped to secure the treaty veto on Austrian union with Germany and she encouraged the formation of the 'Little Entente' of Czechoslovakia, Yugoslavia, and Roumania. Her first alliance with a Little Entente power, concluded in January 1924, was with the one whose strategic position, as Hitler would realise, was most important: Czechoslovakia. The new Czech state defended the approach routes to the Danubian plain from north-east Germany and was economically the strongest member of the Little Entente. The Franco-Czech treaty, like the Franco-Polish, provided for immediate mutual aid in case of unprovoked German attack. Two years later France followed up this alliance by a treaty with Roumania and in November 1927 by one with Yugoslavia.

Thus, by the end of 1927, the chain of alliances was complete. Unfortunately it had three weaknesses. Although Poland also had an alliance with Roumania, her relations with Czechoslovakia were cool because of a dispute over a border district named Teschen and because of Piłsudski's dislike of the Czechs. There was a weak link in the chain at a crucial point. Secondly, while there were strong bonds of interest between France and her allies, they also had divergent preoccupations which pulled them in different directions: Roumania feared Russia above all, Yugoslavia had a history of friction with Italy, and Frenchmen in general tended to be exclusively obsessed with the defence of their own Rhineland frontier. Thirdly, all France's allies, not excluding Poland, were relatively weak. Some of them contained alien minorities, and Yugoslavia and Roumania in particular were economically backward. France gave some of them financial aid, but much of this was directed to strengthening their armaments rather than their economies. Moreover, since she was so much the preponderant partner, the strength of the system would in the last resort depend upon France's real power and determination to maintain it. But France's will to take offensive action had already been sapped by the failure of the Ruhr enterprise. The system would eventually collapse under the political pressure and armed might of

Right: *Diplomatic success for France—Polish head of state Pilsudski in Paris to sign the 1921 treaty of mutual assistance*

Bismarck's depraved successors, the aggressive leaders of National Socialist Germany.

Meanwhile the advent of the *Cartel* to power in 1924 had heralded a less intransigent French approach to international problems. At the same time, as a result of the acceptance of the Dawes Plan at the London Conference in August, the problems of disarmament and of security under the protection or within the framework of the League of Nations had begun to overshadow those of reparation.

The Dawes Plan provided for a reduced and graduated scale of reparation annuities. It also contributed to the restoration of German prosperity, which was an essential prerequisite to the improvement of the political climate, by providing for a large loan to Germany and the reorganisation of the German state bank. It came into operation in October 1924 and worked with remarkable smoothness until May 1930. Agreement had been all the easier because there were now new men in power in London as well as Paris. When Herriot went to the London Conference he found as his opposite number Britain's first Labour Prime Minister, Ramsay MacDonald, who had assumed office after the Conservatives lost the election of December 1923. Both were men of the Left who talked much the same language. Moreover, both were eager to restore good relations between their countries and, as they smoked their pipes at Chequers, the British Prime Minister's country house, they established a personal friendship. When the London Conference came to an end the *Cartel's* newspapers claimed that it was the first time that a conference had strengthened Anglo-French relationships instead of embittering them.

This did not mean that Herriot succeeded in obtaining all he wanted. He showed his conciliatory disposition by bringing French policy more into line with British and by at last according recognition to the Soviet government. He also agreed to fix a date for the evacuation of the Ruhr and the last French and Belgian troops left the territory a year later, in August 1925. But he was unable to make evacuation conditional on France's satisfaction that Germany was complying with the treaty's stipulations on disarmament. This failure was sharply attacked

Right: *A doubly ironical Swiss comment (1927) ridiculing the grotesqueness not of German ambitions but of French fears of German ambitions. The French spokesman declaims: 'They have eaten our children and they will eat them again, so every day we must be on our guard.'* **Next page:** *French cartoon on the crisis of the franc, 1926—Little Red Riding Hood among the wolfish financial ministers.* **Page 96:** *Swiss magazine portrays the ghost of disarmament in May 1928 in a ferocious new disguise—much changed from the spirit of Locarno*

N'OUBLIONS
PAS!

MILLE FRANCS
1.000 FRA

Nebelspalter

rschach, 4. Mai 1928

54. Jahrgang Nr. 1

Die vorbereitende Abrüstungskonferenz

René Gilsi

Und der Geist der Abrüstung erschien. Aber er hatte sich seit Locarno so verändert, dass ihn nur Eingeweihte wieder erkannten.

by Poincaré when the London agreements came up for ratification. But, though Germany consistently and cleverly evaded her disarmament obligations, France's policy of exacting a territorial guarantee to force her to fulfil the treaty had been discredited by the Ruhr episode. She had to look to other means to reinforce her security. One of these was to try and strengthen the League of Nations.

French attempts to strengthen the League

The object of the League, as set out in its Covenant incorporated in each of the post-war peace treaties, was indeed to establish peace and security. Its members undertook to respect one another's 'territorial integrity and political independence' and to treat any war or threat of war as a matter of common concern. But, in spite of provision for economic sanctions, should a member state resort to war, there was no effective machinery to enforce these pious declarations of principle. Moreover, three important powers, the United States, Soviet Russia, and Germany, did not belong to the League. It was no wonder that in France large sections of public opinion were lukewarm or hostile towards it. The conservatives tended to be cool or suspicious. The *Action Française* denounced it as impotent and dangerous, while the Communists condemned it as a piece of bourgeois camouflage. But, although the ordinary Socialist and Radical voter was largely indifferent, the party leaders of the Left and some trade-union chiefs were its fervent supporters. It was therefore natural that when the *Cartel* came into power the League of Nations would loom larger in France's foreign policy.

French diplomacy had already attempted to persuade Britain and other member states to make the League more effective, but its efforts had generally foundered on the rock of British opposition. Now, in 1924, Franco-British differences were reconciled in the so-called Geneva Protocol for the Pacific Settlement of International Disputes. The Covenant had bound member states to resort to one of three different means of resolving disputes likely to end in war. One of these was arbitration, and this emerged as the key factor in the new proposal which the French and British Prime Ministers jointly sponsored. No heads of government of any of the great powers had previously attended a meeting of the League's Assembly, but in September Herriot and MacDonald both went to Geneva, thereby conferring upon the organisation a prestige which it sorely needed. They presented a joint resolution which provided for compulsory arbitration. This, it was believed, would close the 'gaps' in the Covenant, since all disputes must in the last resort be settled by arbitrators whose decision would be final: 'in short, arbitration would make possible security, and security would then lead to disarmament'. The aggressor would be the state which refused to accept arbitration or the verdict of the arbitrators and sanctions would automatically be enforced against it. There was general enthusiasm for this plan which was unanimously adopted by the Assembly and quickly ratified by the French and many other governments. Yet, despite MacDonald's part in sponsoring the Protocol, London was once again the stumbling-block. MacDonald's government, already in a shaky position, fell in November and the Conservative party returned to power. The British dominions, loth to be involved in distant disputes, raised objections, as they had to earlier schemes, and in March 1926 Austen Chamberlain, the new British Foreign Secretary, announced Britain's rejection of the Protocol. Great hopes were buried with that rejection. At Geneva one member of the French delegation later wrote that people used to speak of the year of the Protocol 'as they would talk of great vintage wines'. Herriot, bitterly disappointed, was said to have told Chamberlain that Germany would be at war with Britain in ten years' time. His bitterness was the more understandable since he, like Clemenceau earlier, was vociferously accused by the Nationalist Right of having further sacrificed France's security.

In the following month Herriot too fell from power. The man whom his successor, Painlevé, appointed to the Ministry of Foreign Affairs was Briand, who had already played a part in the French delegation to the League of Nations. He would remain in control of French foreign policy almost without a break until his resignation in 1932. Only one previous Foreign Minister of the Third Republic exceeded him in length of tenure. Government instability did not always mean fluctuations of policy and Briand's nomination signified the continuation of Herriot's conciliatory line. Far more than Herriot he was the European statesman who in the second half of the twenties stood out as the high priest of a new era of hope. That era, all too brief, was symbolised by what came to be called 'the spirit of Locarno' and by the Kellogg Peace Pact of 1928.

The British Conservative government, headed once more by Stanley Baldwin, had rejected the Geneva Protocol, but Chamberlain, the Foreign Secretary, was none the less a francophile, ready to revive the idea of a Franco-British defensive alliance. But the astute Strese-

Right: *International high point, or 'absurd buffoonery' (Clemenceau)? US Secretary of State Kellogg signs the 1928 Kellogg Pact in the glittering Salon de l'Horloge of the Quai d'Orsay*

mann, who directed German foreign policy until his death in 1929, quickly saw that a security agreement without Germany would be an agreement against her. Therefore, even before the official demise of the Geneva Protocol, he proposed that the powers interested in security in the West should enter into a pact not to make war upon one another. Despite the scepticism and reserve of some sections of French opinion, dismayed by the election in the spring of an aged soldier and hero of the former German army, Field Marshal Hindenburg, as German President, Briand readily responded. In the ensuing negotiations he was warmly supported by Chamberlain with whom he established a friendly relationship similar to that of Herriot and MacDonald. The upshot was a subordination of the old idea of a Franco-British alliance to the new one of a Rhineland agreement which would be brought 'within the framework' of the League of Nations. In October 1925 the representatives of the interested powers – Briand with his drooping moustache and cigarette, Stresemann, smooth-faced and shaven-headed, Austen Chamberlain, elegant and monocled, Mussolini, the bull-necked Fascist dictator who had left Italy for the first time since his assumption of power, and the Belgian Vandervelde, small, dark, and lively – gathered together in the town hall of Locarno, a Swiss resort on Lake Maggiore. There, on 16th October they signed the Locarno Pact of Mutual Guarantee whereby they severally and collectively guaranteed both the treaty frontiers between France and Belgium on the one hand and Germany on the other and the provisions governing the demilitarised zone in the Rhineland. The agreement, shown to the waiting crowds in the square below from a lighted window, also provided for Germany's admission to the League of Nations. It was hailed throughout the world as a great step forward. The main problems arising from the war seemed at last to have been resolved and Europe, as Churchill later wrote, emerged into 'the pale sunlight of Locarno'.

Germany re-enters the fold

The 'spirit of Locarno' thus appeared to suffuse a new era of mutual understanding. Germany had negotiated freely. When she entered the League as an equal member in September 1926 she was welcomed by Briand in a moving speech in which he declared, 'Like individuals who go and settle their differences before the magistrate we too will settle ours by peaceful processes. Away with rifles, machine guns and cannon; make room for arbitration and peace!' He and the Germans, he said, had talked together as Europeans, and he and Stresemann alike appeared to be bent on Franco-German reconciliation.

LE FORGERO
— C'est pour la paix q

In 1926 they were both awarded Nobel Peace Prizes and, in September in an intimate meeting in an inn at Thoiry near the Franco-Swiss frontier, they also talked of economic co-operation. In the same year too the Assembly of the League of Nations set up a commission to prepare for a great conference on disarmament and, as witness to the new spirit of fraternity, Soviet representatives were admitted to take part although Russia was not yet a member of the League. Briand, now the maestro who marvellously swayed the League with his musical oratory, extended too his hand of friendship across the Atlantic to another great non-member state, the United States. In April 1927, in a message to the American people on the tenth anniversary of their entry into the war, he declared France's readiness to conclude an agreement 'outlawing' war between them. This was the sort of declaration to move an emotional transatlantic opinion and Kellogg, the American Secretary of State, responded and improved on the proposal. Such an agreement should not be a purely Franco-American affair. It should be open to all powers of good will to subscribe to it.

Some months later, on 27th August 1928, the Kellogg Pact was solemnly signed in the *Salon de l'Horloge* of the Quai d'Orsay in Paris, headquarters of the Ministry of Foreign Affairs, by the representatives of fifteen states. It was eventually adhered to by sixty-three different nations, who thereby, subject to some reservations, renounced war as an instrument of national policy. Having no built-in sanctions, the Pact was no more than another splendid assertion of pious intentions – Clemenceau in his retirement growled that it was an 'absurd buffoonery' – but its signature was the high-water mark of the tide of international euphoria which Briand had done so much to set in motion. It was fitting that this was the year in which the French government reduced the term of military service from eighteen to twelve months. In a notable caricature two years later Briand could with good reason be depicted as 'the blacksmith of peace'.

Yet the sunlight of Locarno was pale and France's real power was diminishing as that of Germany recovered. To the British Ambassador in Berlin who had played an important part in the Locarno negotiations, it seemed that French hegemony was at an end and that the balance of power had been re-established. Locarno no doubt strengthened the peace settlement morally but it enfeebled it materially. It appeared a great achievement to induce Germany freely to accept the Western frontiers, but she would enter into no such obligation in the East.

Left: *'The angels of Locarno' (German cartoon) and 'the blacksmith of peace' (Briand) – but the era of illusions was ending*

This was the weak part of the Locarno arrangements. Britain would not commit herself in Eastern Europe and all Briand's efforts to induce Stresemann to give an undertaking that Germany would not attack her Eastern allies were unavailing. Germany, in fact, was a revisionist power and Stresemann himself said both that he saw in Locarno 'the possibility of recovering German territory in the East' and that membership of the League did not exclude the possibility of war. It was not surprising that Clemenceau asserted that the spirit of Locarno was directly harmful to French interests or that some of France's friends in the East, particularly the Poles, looked at it askance and saw in it a weakening of the 'French system'. The weakening went further when a new Russo-German treaty of friendship was signed in April 1926, and when, in the same year, the Allies evacuated the Cologne zone in the Rhineland, despite Germany's continued evasion of her disarmament obligations. But, for the time being, such a concession seemed an additional contribution to the ending of the age-old Franco-German rivalry. Indeed Briand went even further and toyed with the idea of cementing Franco-German friendship by a grand gesture which would involve the immediate return of the Saarland to Germany and evacuation of the rest of the Rhineland. But French opinion was not ready for such sweeping concessions and all Briand's magic could not have persuaded his countrymen to such magnanimity. As it was, there were too many people in France who believed that Germany was ungrateful for all the concessions already made to her and too many in Germany who believed that France would give nothing away except when compelled to by British and American pressure or her own economic difficulties. Despite all Briand's efforts and all the flowery speeches at Geneva and elsewhere, the new-found Franco-German amity was but skin deep. It would have needed far more men of determination and good will on both sides to make it a reality. But blindness to the depth of French distrust and the continuance of German militarism was characteristic of this 'era of illusions'. And the illusions were more easily cherished because of the return of prosperity after economic crisis.

Left: *German police stand where once French soldiers stood—above Koblenz, 1929. The Rhineland occupation ended in 1930*

Chapter 7

Prosperity Returns

On Armistice Day 1927 the Minister of Public Works, André Tardieu, announced that reconstruction was complete. He was a little premature. It would take another four years to restore all the destroyed or damaged dwelling houses and farm and public buildings. But so far as concerned industry and roads and railways he was virtually correct. And by then most of the villages and towns of north-eastern France had risen anew. Factories were humming, coalmines were in full production, and farmers were again rearing cattle and producing such valuable cash crops as wheat, sugar beet, and flax. The great task, which by 1931 had cost about 100 milliard francs, has been described as the most impressive economic achievement of the inter-war years; it was carried out by Frenchmen and immigrants, chiefly from Allied countries, since Germany's offer of labour was spurned for nationalist reasons by French and other contractors.

The return of prosperity to the north-east, traditionally one of the wealthier areas, was reflected throughout the country. Although the flight from the land continued and agriculture remained inefficient in many areas, France again ranked high as a grower of wheat, only coming behind far bigger countries such as India, Russia, Canada, and the United States. By 1929, mainly because of the growth of large-scale farming in the north-east, the average yield per acre had increased by thirty per cent since 1914. She was, moreover, foremost again in wine production and her depleted livestock had been reconstituted.

But it was mining and industry that were the most dynamic sectors of the economy and there France's achievements were often remarkable. In conformity with a widespread pattern in industrialised countries the more enterprising concerns, especially in the Paris area and the north and east, began to rationalise the employment of labour, concentrate production, and standardise parts. The regaining of the Lorraine iron field, the second biggest in the world, gave a great im-

***Left:** Mass production comes to France—Citroën factory 1932*

France's balance of payments 1919-34 Figures in millions of francs

The franc, in relation to the dollar

(Par : 5.18 fr)
1928 devaluation : par 25.52 fr

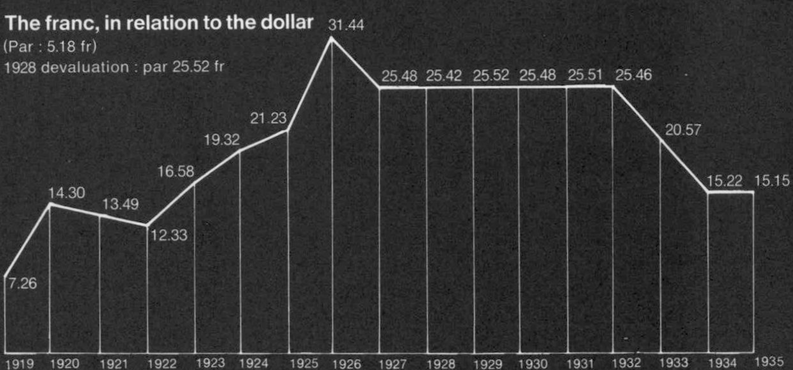

The progress of reconstruction Percentage of reconstruction on 1914 figures

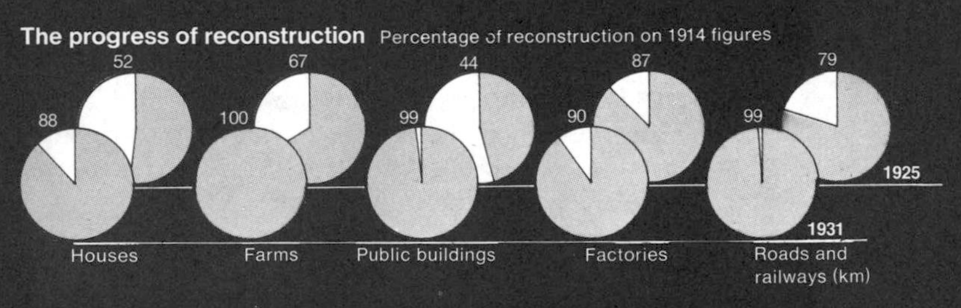

World output of pig iron 1925 Figures in thousands of tons

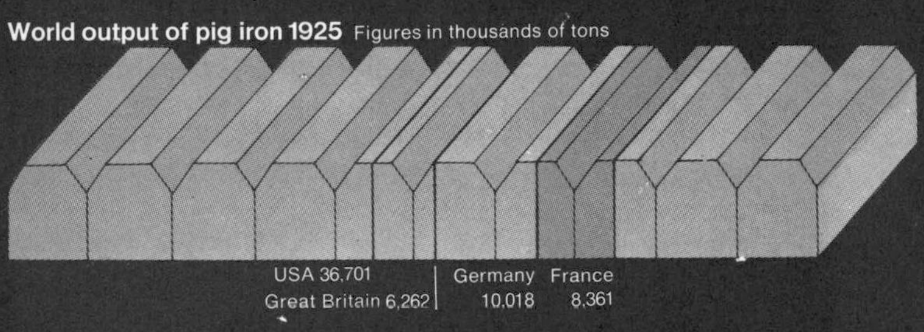

World output of steel 1925 Figures in thousands of tons

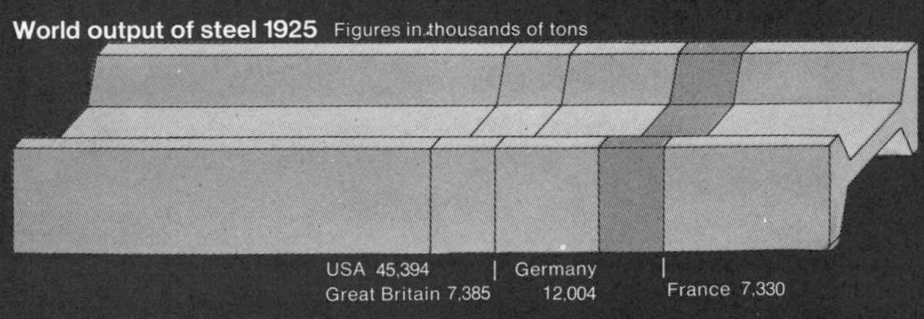

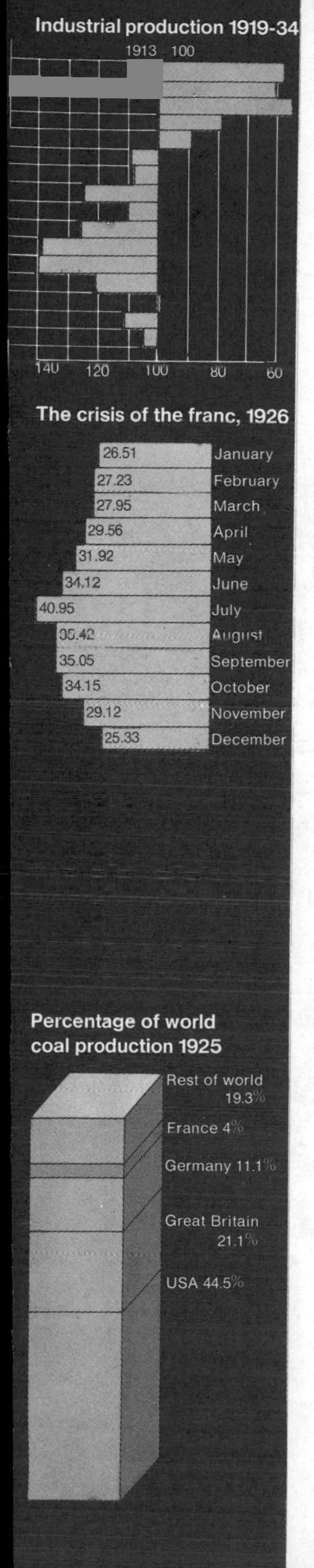

petus to steel production and France exported larger quantities than ever before both of iron ore and finished steel. In the Parisian region car production went ahead with the growth of such firms as Citroën, Renault, and Peugeot: by 1928 output reached 2,600,000 cars a year and France was a leader in making inexpensive vehicles. André Citroën, in particular, was a new type of French manufacturer who imitated American mass production and advertising methods with their drive and vulgarity. He boosted his firm by skywriting and illuminated signs on the Eiffel Tower. In the south, where France was the greatest European producer of bauxite, the aluminium industry forged ahead and, among others, gave notable impetus to hydro-electric development in the Alps, the Pyrenees, and the Massif Central, while in the east the recovery of Alsace strengthened her woollen industry and made her once more a large cotton producer. Her chemical industries in general made striking progress, but it was in Alsace too that she became one of the foremost European producers of potash. In Alsace also there was a new venture, the development of oil drilling at Péchelbronn, although this made a very small contribution to France's needs of crude oil which had mainly to be imported. But elsewhere she began to develop oil refineries. In 1920 the value of the country's total imports had been nearly double that of exports: by 1924 the value of exports had almost doubled and exceeded that of imports. All these advances were facilitated by the extension of credit and banking services, often with state support. Moreover, France continued to be one of the world's chief financial lenders and a centre of the international money market.

This economic prosperity of the later twenties was furthered by improvements in communications. Although the railways were embarrassed by rising costs and the increasing competition of motor transport, a number of lines were electrified and new services were provided in dock areas. The river port of Strasbourg was on the way to becoming a great centre of traffic. The seaports of Dunkirk, Le Havre, Saint-Nazaire, and Bordeaux were adapted to deal with larger ships and an increasing volume of trade and, although much of this was carried in foreign vessels, by 1925 the tonnage of the merchant navy had risen from the ninth place it had occupied in the world table in 1908 to the fourth. At the same time the great increase in tourists from overseas – in 1925 there were nearly 500,000 British visitors and 200,000

***Left:** Diagrams illustrating the movement of the franc in the mid twenties, the progress of post-war reconstruction, and the changing economic pattern of the balance of payments*

SENNEP

Americans – provided an added incentive to the enlargement of ports such as Cherbourg. Tourists had indeed come to France for decades, but now, as never before, they were an important source of revenue. For the wealthier women dressmaking houses were as ever a magnet, while many, wealthy or not, who visited the Paris Exhibition of Decorative Arts in 1925, must have been impressed by French ingenuity and the quality of French products.

These were the products of an economy in which virtually all hands were at work. In 1926 there were only 585 unemployed in receipt of relief. With the help of some three million immigrant workers, average industrial productivity had increased by thirty-one per cent since 1913. In 1929 average overall productivity had increased by thirty-eight per cent despite the reduction of working hours.

This new-found prosperity was reflected in living standards. A number of firms took pains to house their workers better, and the growing adoption of the English week-end gave many people more leisure. Moreover, as there was now a greater variety of alluring goods or services available to the consumer, bread and other foodstuffs played a smaller part in the family budget. Bicycles and cars were objects of desire and many a franc would go on the use of automatic telephones – introduced in 1928 – or on seats at the cinema (where, until the late twenties, films were still silent) or on that great new toy, the wireless set. Happily for the wage-earner his purchasing power had increased by 1930, although the improvement varied widely according to occupation. Thus, for an employee of the state tobacco monopoly the increase since 1914 was only about two per cent, whereas for unskilled labourers in the provinces it was twenty-six per cent. Overall the living standard of the average Frenchman had by the end of the twenties increased by thirty-three per cent. Moreover, now that sport was attracting an unprecedented degree of interest and publicity, his sense of well-being and national pride could be vicariously enhanced by the exploits of such brilliant tennis players as Suzanne Lenglen and the Davis cup winners, Cochet, Lacoste, Brugnon, and Borotra. He could rejoice in the victories of French athletes in the Olympic Games, or of rugby and association football players over various rival teams from the British Isles. He could glow at the achievements of French aviators, such as Saint-Exupéry

Top left: *The crisis of the franc, 1926; Sennep's view of French bankruptcy – all that's left in the safe is Poincaré; and* Punch *cartoon – the taxpayer tells Finance Minister Doumer: 'I'll do anything in reason, but I won't shove!'* ***Bottom:*** *Street reactions*

and Mermoz (who developed long-distance services) and Costes and Le Brix, famed for their journey in 1928 from Paris to Washington by way of Africa and South America.

Poincaré to the rescue

The sense of returning prosperity had, of course, been temporarily checked by the financial crisis which caused such alarm in 1926. Its termination gave a new fillip to France's economy. Herriot, it will be remembered, had fallen on 21st July and shortly before his fall the franc had tumbled to 243 to the £. A saviour was needed, someone who would restore financial confidence no matter what the colour of his politics. Fortunately such a man was at last to hand. The politicians of the *Cartel* had played themselves out and Doumergue could look elsewhere. He called on Poincaré and the mere news that Poincaré had been invited to form a government caused the franc to rise to 220 to the £.

The reappearance of the sexagenarian whose Ruhr policy had been such a failure and who had been so attacked nearly two and a half years earlier might seem surprising. But Poincaré had retained his prestige as a man of patriotism and integrity: his Republicanism was unimpeachable, he had preserved his reputation for efficiency and financial competence, and he had carefully disengaged himself from too close association with the Right and its hostility to the *Cartel*. Moreover, when his recent enemies got into difficulties he had refrained from humiliating them. He thus inspired confidence. Although he could not bring about a national union government of members of all the main parliamentary groups (except the Communists) because the Socialists once again refused to participate, he rapidly formed a cabinet which marked a departure from the normal pattern. It was largely dependent on support from the Centre groups instead of being a Right or Left-wing coalition supported by a fraction of the Centre. The new government was none the less impressive. It was small, containing only thirteen ministers, but they included Herriot and four other former Prime Ministers, apart from Poincaré. It clearly meant business and, while he gave the political posts to the Left Centre and economic ones to the Right Centre, Poincaré himself took the Ministry of Finance as well as the Premiership. When he and his colleagues first faced the Chamber on 27th July the Communists made noisy scenes, at one time sing-

Left: *'Le sport' becomes French—Antonin Magne, winner of the 1931 Tour de France, Suzanne Lenglen* ***(top left)****, the aviator Saint-Exupéry, with his sturdy mechanic* ***(bottom left)***

ing the *Internationale,* and one of them, Marcel Cachin, cried out, 'You are only to be seen in times of misfortune!' Meant as an insult, the remark was a tribute. Poincaré was not a night bird of ill omen; he was seen in such times because men believed that he, if anyone, would put things right.

Poincaré's achievement was a remarkable illustration of the political importance of personality and psychology. Even before he had time to put through any remedial legislation the franc had risen to 196. By November it was back at 130 to the pound. In parliament on 3rd August the deputies who had refused to give special powers to Caillaux granted them to Poincaré; his government was authorised to effect by decree laws 'all the economies compatible with the effective functioning of the public services'. The French investor showed that he was again ready to trust his government, provided that he could feel that his recent panic had been due to accidents which would not recur.

The rapid recovery of the franc meant that before long Poincaré could achieve a further aim and informally stabilise it at a new level. In December he decided on this and thenceforward the Bank of France bought foreign currency at the rate of 124 francs to the pound. But once the franc had thus been preserved and financial stability restored a further question arose. Should it be revalued or devalued? This was the subject of protracted debate. Revaluation meant, in one of the popular phrases of the time, 'reconducting the pound as far as the frontier' or returning to the pre-war rate of 25 francs to the pound. Devaluation meant amputating the old franc by four-fifths and formally stabilising the exchange at approximately its existing level. Those who favoured the former believed it was essential for France's honour, prestige, and credit to restore the old monetary order; those who opposed it did so for many reasons, one in particular being that the progressive revaluing necessary before the franc could return to its pre-war level would involve further uncertainty and speculation—what the country needed was order there and then. But it was for Poincaré to decide. No one portrayed the situation better than the celebrated caricaturist Sennep, who depicted France's notables as a procession of Egyptian dignitaries seen in profile and winding their way towards the deity at the summit: Poincaré, the Sphinx. And with supreme astute-

Right: *Commercial art 1931—a toothpaste advertisement symbolises the new spirit of prosperity.* ***Next page:*** *'Le weekend' enters the French vocabulary, in the form of a country-house car rally* ***(left)****, while 'une vraie parisienne' samples the new freedom* ***(right).*** ***Page 116:*** *Pullman train advertisement*

RENON '33
SÉRODENT
SÉRODENT
la santé des dents
CLERMONT ET FOUET
PARIS
GENÈVE
AFFICHES S.A.P.A. GENÈVE

guy
sabran

La Vie Parisienne

Samedi 23 Novembre 1929
67e ANNÉE Nº 47 — PRIX : 3 fr. 00

CE QU'IL EST CONVENU D'APPELER : UNE VRAIE PARISIENNE.

CHEMIN DE FER DU NORD
A.M. CASSANDRE 27
HACHARD & Cie PARIS.
NEDERLANDSCHE SPOORWEGEN
SOCIETE NATIONALE DES CHEMINS DE FER BELGES
ÉTOILE DU NORD
DU DÉJEUNER
PULLMAN
AU DINER
PARIS—BRUXELLES—AMSTERDAM
OMPAGNIE DES WAGONS-

ness Poincaré *was* a Sphinx. He watched and waited and refused to be hustled into a hasty decision. The men of the *Cartel* had constantly been overtaken by events, the rapid succession of ministers had had no time for reflection. But Poincaré bided his time and, moreover, waited until in the elections of 1928 the nation as a whole had given him a vote of confidence. It was not until June of that year that the man who was temperamentally a traditionalist in favour of revaluation pronounced for devaluation and the formal stabilisation of the franc at 125 to the £. The old *'franc germinal'* of 1803 had gone for ever. It was replaced by the 'franc at five sous'. It has been said by a French economic historian that of all the great financial decisions taken between the two wars this was almost the only one that was not a blunder. It was Poincaré's culminating achievement and the climax of the return to financial stability. The sun of economic prosperity shone more warmly than ever. The franc had been preserved, if not restored to pre-war parity. No one dreamed of the great storm clouds that before long would gather across the Atlantic and move eastward with the force of a hurricane.

The storm clouds gather

The Poincaré government lasted longer than any other between 1918 and 1934. It held office for more than two years and, while Poincaré set the finances to rights and Briand pursued his role as the pilgrim of peace, France enjoyed a political calm virtually undisturbed save by the activities of extremists and by some of those financial scandals which periodically punctuated the history of the Third Republic. On the extreme Right the *Action Française* had met with discomfiture while on the extreme Left, Communist manifestations were firmly repressed.

The nationalist *Action Française* deserves note as much for its extraordinary intellectual influence as for its direct role in politics, although there too it had a disintegrating influence. Monarchist and Catholic, it was dominated by two men: a remarkable deaf journalist, Charles Maurras, and the turbulent Léon Daudet, son of the well-known author Alphonse Daudet. Maurras was editor of its virulently polemical newspaper, the *Action Française,* and through this and his other writings he built up a body of seemingly coherent doctrines which had a strong appeal to a series of talented writers, as well as to many young intellectuals, disillusioned with the regime. But the movement's monarchism and Catholicism were both unorthodox. It advocated monarchy as a form of strong government, not because it had an unswerving devotion to the Orleanist pretender; it sought Catholic support because it saw in the Church a force making for

order and not because its leaders were devout believers —Maurras himself was an agnostic. So it attempted to exploit the Church for its own purposes and had early become suspect to Rome. Already in 1914 Pope Pius X had approved a decree placing five of Maurras' works on the Index, but its publication had been deferred. Now in 1926 Pius XI, encouraged by Briand who represented the movement as an obstacle to religious pacification in France, not only promulgated the decree, but also condemned the *Action Française* newspaper. Catholics were forbidden to read it and before long those who persisted in doing so were to be deprived of the sacraments.

Although many of its Catholic adherents defied the ban, the movement was permanently weakened by Rome's drastic action and its membership sharply declined. Before long it was but one of a growing number of anti-parliamentary leagues whose existence added confusion and turbulence to the political scene of the thirties. Yet its violent propaganda against Jews, foreigners, freemasons, and others whom it regarded as harmful alien bodies in the French nation, together with the violent methods of its youth organisation, the *Camelots du Roi,* were disturbing factors. They helped to weaken the forces of liberalism in the inter-war years.

On the extreme Left the Communists were untouched by 'French socialism's deep-rooted humanitarian and libertarian heritage'. Under the ruthless direction of Moscow and the auspices of younger and more proletarian leaders they had been reorganising. One such was Maurice Thorez, a miner's son, who in 1930 became the general secretary of the party, and its activities gained a new impetus from France's recognition of the USSR. The old departmental organisations were replaced by larger regional groupings and the formation of cells of party members in factories and districts became a prime objective. By 1925 the party had won Moscow's approval for its agitation against the Moroccan war and in January 1927, when two Italian anarchists, Sacco and Vanzetti, originally arrested in Boston, Massachusetts in 1921, were executed, it organised violent demonstrations in Paris. A number of shops on the main boulevards were sacked. The repression was severe but these growing Communist activities had an important political consequence. They were a factor in causing parliament to alter the electoral law.

New elections were due in 1928, and many deputies

Left: *The 1925 Paris Exhibition of Decorative Arts gave birth to the term 'Art Deco'—a lively ornamental style popular in the twenties and thirties.* ***Top:*** *A glass-panelled studio in the Exhibition.* ***Bottom:*** *Edgar Brandt's metallic screen 'The Oasis'* feared that the existing electoral system would lead to an increase in Communist representation. The Radicals and Socialists wanted to return to the old system of voting for a single candidate in a smaller constituency. The Radical Minister of the Interior, Albert Sarraut, raised the cry of 'Communism, there is the enemy!', and the new measure was voted into law in July 1927. It was a popular measure. There were more candidates and a heavier poll then ever before and, although on the first ballot the Communists for the first time polled more than a million votes, they had only fourteen deputies in the new Chamber compared with twenty-six in the old. Thorez himself was defeated. Their increased poll had scared many and reinforced the moderate vote on the second ballot. Moreover, their offer to form a 'workers' bloc' with the Socialists had been scornfully rejected. The mutual hatred of the two Left-wing parties continued and the result was an endorsement of government by the Centre. Above all it was a vote of confidence in Poincaré.

Poincaré was naturally called upon to form the new government and he made few changes. But it did not last long. The Radical Socialists were restive and eager, in a well-known phrase, 'to take a cure in opposition'. One of their ablest men, Caillaux, jealous of Poincaré and embittered at having been kept out of office, brought about the cabinet's fall. Its finance bill included, with doubtful propriety, a provision allowing French religious congregations teaching abroad to set up houses in France. Here, in the eyes of many of the Left, the cloven hoof of clericalism was showing itself again – and here was Caillaux's chance. When the Radical ministers left the party congress at Angers in October 1928 and returned to Paris before it ended, he persuaded the party in their absence to censure the government and invite the Radical ministers to resign. They promptly complied and Poincaré had to form another cabinet which was more homogeneous but more to the Right. 'In the streets,' wrote André Siegfried, 'order was kept more strictly and on the official platforms there were more Cardinals.'

The man who, along with the Prefect of Police, was responsible for order was the new Minister of the Interior, André Tardieu, formerly a brilliant henchman of Clemenceau. Scintillating, arrogant, and authoritarian, he proved a powerful hammerer of the Communists. To prevent large-scale Communist manifestations on May Day 1929 the police made more than 4,000 preventive arrests. Later, when the Communist International decreed that 1st August should be universally observed as a 'red

Right: *Posters in the 1928 electoral campaign denounce the evils of Communism. But the Party won over a million votes*

PALACE
COMMUNISTE EST UN PARTI D'ASSASSINS
MMUNISME C'EST LE RÈGNE DU CRIME
PALACE
AUX NUES!
SPADARO
DAMIA
PALACE
PALACE
NUES!
LE NOUVEAU CARTEL
POINCARÉ

international day' of anti-war demonstrations and when the French party proclaimed it 'a day in which the streets were to be conquered by and for the working class', the arrests were still more widespread. Thorez himself was seized and imprisoned for nearly a year. On 1st August, instead of the 250,000 workers hoped for by the Communist leaders, only 7,000 came out to demonstrate. The Party was cowed and soon reached a new low ebb: by mid-1930 membership had dropped from 55,000 to 38,000 and the circulation of *L'Humanité* had fallen. In the autumn of that year Thorez was again defeated, this time in a Paris bye-election. Yet he claimed that this election was a turning point, since it marked a new departure in policy. Now the directive was: 'to struggle more vigorously than ever against all Socialist organisations; but to stretch out a hand and form a single front with the Socialist workers'. Much was to be heard of this single front, or *front unique,* in the following years.

Meanwhile, an event occurred which, with others, symbolised the ending of an era. Poincaré had to resign because of ill-health. It was the close of his political career and he died five years later. His reputation was untarnished and his ascendancy still such that his successor Briand, who remained at the Ministry of Foreign Affairs, kept Poincaré's cabinet. Continuity in the Poincaré tradition was for the moment the order of the day; but it was a shortlived ideal. The 1928 parliament had still nearly three years to go, but during that period there were no fewer than nine different cabinets. New men were now coming to the fore. Tardieu himself headed three cabinets, and in 1931 the rising and adroit politician Pierre Laval formed a ministry for the first time. In the same year there was a Presidential election. Doumergue's term of office ended and he was succeeded by the septuagenarian President of the Senate, Paul Doumer, an austere and rather forbidding old man who had lost three sons in the war. But the man Doumer defeated was Aristide Briand who, with Poincaré, had dominated French politics in the twenties more than any other politician. Briand's defeat, engineered by Laval and others, was also a symbol. The policies for which he stood were gradually being discredited, above all by disquieting events in Germany. The 'era of illusions' was ending and the pale sunlight of Locarno was receding towards the horizon. Meanwhile, his German counterpart Stresemann had died in October 1929 and

Left: *One of the last attempts at Franco-German rapprochement before the Nazis came to power: a meeting in July 1931 between (front row l. to r.) French Foreign Minister Briand, Henderson (UK), Laval, Stimson (US), and Chancellor Brüning of Germany*

in the same year two other great figures had departed from the scene, Foch and Clemenceau. Whereas Foch's body was borne in state to the Arc de Triomphe, Clemenceau, like General de Gaulle forty-one years later, would have no great Parisian funeral—'neither manifestations, nor invitations, nor rites'. In accordance with his wishes he was buried with the utmost simplicity in a remote village in his native Vendée.

The first rumblings of depression

The first big storm cloud gathered far away across the Atlantic with the Wall Street crash of Black Thursday, 24th October 1929. It was the beginning of the great depression. Yet, although purchasing power had begun to decline and raw material prices to fall after February, no one in France thought that the American slump would have world-wide and shattering repercussions. Industrial production increased until 1930. The country's relatively backward economic structure cushioned it from the sort of economic cataclysm which hit the United States, Germany, and Britain, and the luck of a bad harvest in 1930 staved off the problem of agricultural surpluses which was such a trouble elsewhere. Devaluation had made France a cheap country for foreign purchasers and tourists. The franc was stable and her gold reserves continued to rise. In 1930, when Britain had well over 2 million unemployed and Germany more than 3 million, France, with less than 300,000, appeared to be a happy island in a ravaged world. Meanwhile, as if to emphasise her felicity, her new men at the end of 1929 had inaugurated what they called 'a policy of prosperity'. Five milliards were to be spent 'to accelerate the nation's equipment'.

This new policy of spending part of the 'treasure' accumulated by Poincaré and his successor at the Ministry of Finance was a startling move for a Right-wing government. Agriculture, industry and commerce, health and education were all intended to benefit from this unexpected largesse. The motives and measures were partly demagogic, but at last there was also some social reform. A new school-building programme was launched and, despite traditional Catholic opposition, fees were abolished in the highest forms of *Lycées*—a first step towards free secondary education. A social insurance law, long urged by the Socialists and CGT, was passed in 1930 and family allowances were introduced in 1932. In May 1930, yielding to pressure from the war veterans' organisation, the *Confédération des Anciens Combattants,* the second Tardieu ministry granted a retirement pension to ex-servicemen over fifty who had spent three months or more at the front. Tardieu had indeed stolen some of the

thunder of the Left and Léon Blum in the *Populaire* voiced his vexation: 'Naturally when . . . we . . . suggested such beneficial irrigation all the reactionary Press was up in arms. . . . They denounced . . . our crazy prodigality . . . we were going to overturn Poincaré's splendid work. . . . Tardieu takes hold of the idea and at once all becomes fine.' In taking hold of the idea Tardieu was in advance of his time. It was not yet common practice in parliamentary democracies for governments to intervene and seek to regulate production by stimulating demand and accepting a budgetary deficit.

But France's labour force was too inelastic to respond significantly, and in an economically interdependent world she could not remain untouched by the ever-broadening financial crisis and economic slump, although it did not begin to make its full impact on her until 1933. The collapse in October 1930 of the Oustric bank in dubious circumstances implicating one of Tardieu's ministers was superficially the kind of financial scandal to which the Third Republic was habituated. But it was symptomatic of a growing malaise. By the end of 1931 the economic situation had patently deteriorated. Unemployment was on the increase, the tourist trade was declining, outlets for foreign trade were closing, wholesale prices had slumped and the government had intervened for the first time to limit production, starting with the vineyards. By then too the general crisis had been accentuated anew because Britain had taken the drastic step of devaluing the pound and abandoning the gold standard. Moreover, Tardieu's demagogic concession to ex-servicemen had saddled his country with a heavy additional burden: 'in 1939 when the second war began one Frenchman in ten was in receipt of a pension or retirement payment on account of the first war'.

Meanwhile, the international situation was also deteriorating, for the depression jeopardised parliamentary governments and gave an impetus to military dictatorships. Here, too, 1930 was a turning point. Yet paradoxically France, because as yet she was relatively immune from economic trouble, appeared for a brief time to be more than ever the strongest power in Europe.

At first the main problems were still the familiar ones of interallied debts, reparation, and disarmament. Back in 1926 a Franco-American agreement had arranged for the payment of France's debt to the United States to be spread over sixty-two years. But the American view that interallied debts and reparation were separate problems was still contested in France and it was not until 1929 that the agreement was ratified by the French parlia-

Left: *First-fruits of depression—a soup-line in Montmartre* ment. Meanwhile, when in 1928 Stresemann had raised the question of the Rhineland, Poincaré and Briand had insisted that this must be linked with reparation, since the Allied occupation was a guarantee of reparation payments and the total amount of Germany's liability and the period over which payment should extend were still undetermined. In 1929, under a new arrangement known as the Young Plan, the scale of payments was again revised downwards and 1988 was fixed as the terminal date. At last the reparation problem appeared to have been settled. The Reparation Commission was dissolved and the Allies agreed to evacuate the Rhineland five years before the date prescribed by the Treaty of Versailles. The demilitarised zone continued to exist, but the last occupying troops had left by 30th June 1930.

Thus two of the thorniest problems bequeathed by the war, interallied debts and reparation, appeared to have been disposed of. There remained the most intractable of all: disarmament. The Preparatory Commission had first met in 1926 but by 1928 it had made no progress, largely owing to divergences of view between Britain and France, who continued to put security before disarmament. It was only in naval matters that some initial advance had been made when, at the Washington Conference in 1921-2, the chief naval powers, including France and Italy, had agreed to a ten years' 'holiday' in the construction of capital ships. But by 1930, when the end of the holiday was nearing and a further conference was held in London, France was meeting with naval competition from Italy, who claimed naval parity with her, and neither power was inclined to conclude a new restrictive agreement. In the same year, however, the Preparatory Commission produced a draft convention and the time at last seemed ripe to call the long-awaited World Disarmament Conference. But when the delegates assembled in Geneva in February 1932 the omens were more unfavourable than ever before. 'Briandism' had broken down and the economic crisis had suspended reparations and brought the Weimar Republic to its last gasp.

At Geneva in 1929, in imaginative pursuit of the will of the wisp of European peace, Briand had spoken of the possibility of a European Union. On 30th June 1930, the day when the Rhineland occupation ended, he had sent a memorandum on the subject to twenty-six governments. But its reception was cool, especially in Italy and in Germany, where the well-known *Deutsche Allgemeine Zeitung* wrote that its author had merely 'transposed

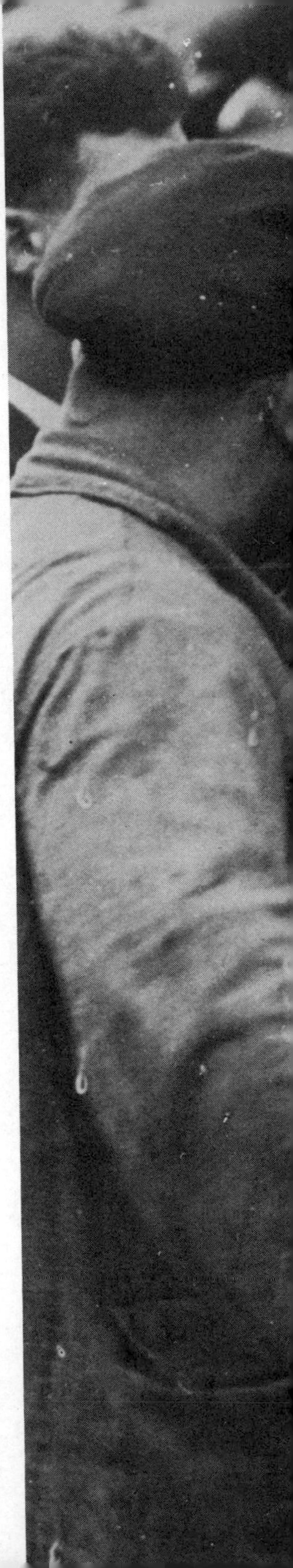

***Right:** Growing violence and disorder accompanied the spread of such Right-wing leagues as the ex-servicemen's* Croix de Feu

the language of French imperialism into a harmonious Esperanto'. In September the League of Nations set up a commission to study Briand's proposal. It was politely buried. Beset by economic difficulties, most European governments had other preoccupations. One was the situation in Germany where elections were held in that same September. A rabidly nationalist party, which had previously polled less than a million votes, won more than six million, and 107 seats in the Reichstag. Henceforward, National-Socialism and its hypnotic leader Adolf Hitler were forces to be reckoned with in Europe as well as in Germany.

In France it was a government of the Right that had agreed to the Rhineland evacuation and governments of the Right which had continued Briand's tenure as foreign minister because of his European prestige. But the debt settlements, the Young Plan, and the evacuation had all met with fierce criticism and these had partly caused the fall of Briand's own cabinet in October 1929. It was no wonder that in March 1931, when Austria and Germany sought to distract attention from their economic difficulties by proclaiming a customs union, France, preoccupied as ever with security, felt bound to oppose it. Economic union was only too likely to lead to the political union vetoed at Versailles. Her opposition prevailed and in September the abandonment of the union was a French political triumph. At much the same time France had improved her relations with the Soviet Union sufficiently to initial a draft Franco-Soviet non-aggression pact, and in March 1932 Tardieu put forward a plan to strengthen the economies of the Little Entente and its neighbours by making the Danube basin a free trade area assisted by a reconstruction loan from France, Britain, Germany, and Italy. French diplomacy appeared more than ever to have the initiative. Moreover, in 1931 France's apparently continuing greatness was emphasised by a splendid colonial exhibition at Vincennes.

It was one of the last great shows of the Third Republic. In January 1932, a few weeks after it closed, Briand resigned and two months later he was dead. With the passing of the 'blacksmith of peace' the era of illusions was finally over and France's diplomatic initiatives would soon be frustrated at almost every turn.

Left: *The image of the amiable father figure—Albert Lebrun, the safe but undistinguished President elected in 1932*

MARCHE
DES CH
DU NOR

Chapter 8

Hard Times

The great depression tended everywhere to precipitate the overthrow of existing governments or regimes. In France, too, it had its impact and the 1932 elections ended government by ministries inclined to the Right. But otherwise the elections were undramatic and in many ways followed a normal pattern showing the French voters' affection for the old ways. Nevertheless, they ushered in a new period of trouble and confusion. As if to herald the dark days ahead, Doumer, the President of the Republic, was assassinated on 6th May by a lunatic Russian named Gorguloff. The assassination took place between the first and second ballots and it was the old Chamber which, with the Senate, elected Doumer's successor. Their choice fell once again on the President of the Senate, now Albert Lebrun. He was a dignified and well-meaning but somewhat colourless figure. But so were many of his predecessors. None of those who voted for him can have dreamt that they were electing the last President of the Third Republic.

In the general election 9,500,000 men turned out to vote: the poll was still heavier than in 1928. The result was both a vote against government by the Right and a protest against the worsening economic situation.

Tardieu had had the misfortune to launch his policy of prosperity on the eve of the biggest depression of modern times. What the elector saw was growing unemployment – business stagnation, a general fall in agricultural prices, and a new cessation of reparation payments. He voted accordingly and the Left-wing groups had a bigger majority than the *Cartel* in 1924.

Yet their relations were less harmonious and people did not even talk of a *Cartel*-type union. Many Socialists, weary of being in the wilderness, had, even in 1929, favoured participating in government when invited to do so by the Radical Daladier. But, although the parliamentary group had voted for participation, the party's national council had rejected it. Now in 1932, as in 1924,

Left: *Hungry coalminers singing the 'Internationale' march through the 'Red suburb' of St Denis in Paris, December 1933*

Herriot was asked to form a government, but the Socialists laid down conditions for participation which some of them probably knew would be unacceptable, and Herriot attacked them as 'revolutionaries in rabbit skins', mockingly quoting a sign which said 'Socialist restaurant, bourgeois cooking'.

Herriot's attitude was dominated by remembrance of his difficulties in 1924-6. Confronted once again by acute financial problems and a budgetary deficit, since Poincaré's 'treasure' had been dissipated, he thought that deflation was the answer. But the Socialists' conditions vetoed deflation and Herriot rejected them out of hand. Once again, while the Socialists gave general support to his other policies, they withheld it on finance. The Right and the Left, on the other hand, took the opposite position, supporting his financial measures but deploring his attitude on other issues. The old dilemma had recurred.

However, when Herriot fell, it was on a question of international, not domestic, finance. Paradoxically the French themselves had contributed to the further deterioration of the international situation in 1931. Their refusal to help the Austrian *Kredit Anstalt* bank had meant that there was a run on German reserves and a withdrawal of short-term funds from London. Then President Hoover had prescribed a year's moratorium on international payments. As a result Britain's own loans were blocked. London, the centre of the international banking system, despite French and American help, had not enough gold to meet the drain on her reserves, and England, as we have seen, had gone off the gold standard and devalued the pound. Before long twelve other countries had followed suit. The international monetary system had broken down. Meanwhile, Germany's new financial and political crisis was rapidly growing worse. In the middle of 1932, when the moratorium was drawing to an end, France and Germany's other creditors, in a desperate effort to save the tottering Weimar Republic, agreed to end reparations in return for a final payment of 3 milliard marks.

This was naturally unpopular in France. Still more unpopular was the Americans' continued insistence on their pound of flesh. Now that international payments had resumed, France was due to pay a further instalment of her war debt to the United States in December. But when

Right: *French life-styles—a poster for the Brittany beach resort of La Baule les Pins (1926).* ***Next page:*** *'Le salon de thé' by Vuillard—a picture of middle-class gentility.* ***Page 136:*** *Preening the image, Paris-fashion—an advertisement from* L'Illustration, *1931, portrays the romance of dressing up*

LA BAULE LES PINS

SON CLIMAT MERVEILLEUX
SES TERRAINS BOISÉS - SA PLAGE

Société Générale Foncière
FACILITÉS DE PAIEMENT

Bureaux de Vent
LA BAULE LES PINS ET
63, BOUL^D MALESHERBES - PARI

E. Vuillard

Herriot urged that payment was a matter of honour, the deputies, including the Socialists, revolted and public opinion was behind them. Herriot's policy was rejected by 402 to 186 and he resigned. It was his last cabinet. Ministerial instability was again the order of the day. Within the next fourteen months there were five different governments. In the mid-twenties men had talked of a 'cascade' of ministries, now they spoke of a 'massacre'.

Omens from Germany

For France the foreign situation had been fast deteriorating. As ever, security and relations with Germany were the crux of the situation. What Germany now demanded was equality of rights or, in other words, the right to re-arm to the level of other powers. But this was as ever objectionable to France with her inferior manpower and industrial resources. Her fear was indeed justified but, apart from her direct allies, there were few statesmen who, like Winston Churchill in 1931, saw that the French army was a stabilising factor, whose sudden weakening 'might open floodgates of measureless consequences'.

Eventually, in September 1932, after months of argument, Germany left the Disarmament Conference. In December she returned when an ambiguous formula recognised the principle both of her equality of rights and of France's right to security. But this concession did not save the Weimar Republic. At the end of January 1933, two days after the fall of another French cabinet, Hitler became the German Chancellor. The Nazis were in power and in October Germany finally left not only the Disarmament Conference but also the League of Nations. Disarmament was dead, the League was a broken reed, and German rearmament, which had been proceeding for years in violation of the Versailles treaty, was soon accelerated.

It was against such a background that the French had chosen to economise on defence. Reduction in government expenditure was a classic measure to meet a deficit and for a Left-wing majority military expenditure was a natural target. So in July 1932 the Chamber had slashed military credits and further cuts would follow.

France's army still appeared the foremost in Europe, but in military as in economic development she was hampered by the past. Control was divided between the Ministry of War, the General Staff, and the newly-created Army Council whose Vice-President was to command in time of war. But the Council was dominated by elderly and complacent generals who thought in terms of 1914-18. Moreover, the army had been a victim of the inflation of the twenties; many officers had resigned their commissions and it was unpopular as a career. These factors, the failure of the Ruhr occupation and successive reductions in size, effected mainly for financial reasons, had led to a decline in morale. In de Gaulle's words: 'the profession of arms . . . lamented its own lost ardour' —it was an army without a mission. To one disillusioned officer the ardour had so far vanished that he entitled a book published in 1929 *Feu l'Armée Française* (The Late French Army). By then the composition of the army too had been modified. In 1928 the term of service had been reduced to twelve months and the gap between the number of conscripts and the total required had to be filled by professionals and an increasing number of colonial troops.

By then too the doctrine that in war with Germany France must rely for victory on a lightning strategic offensive had been discarded. The army's reorganisation had not made it capable of 'driving home an offensive punch'. Dangerously lacking in flexibility, it was 'a slow-moving steam-roller of fire designed to push back gradually, as in 1918, any similar army'. But what if the enemy's army was dissimilar?

This defensive mentality, increasingly apparent after 1923, was in 1929 typified by parliament's decision to construct a great line of casemates along the eastern frontier. Long championed by Painlevé, the line was named after the war minister of the day, André Maginot. But the Maginot Line was planned to cover only the German and Luxemburg frontier and when in 1932 the new Chief-of-Staff, General Weygand, urged that the still largely unconstructed fortifications should be prolonged to the sea his proposal was rejected by Pétain and others. This meant that the line might be turned by an enemy invading through Belgium. The vast sums allocated to it would have been spent in vain.

But the worth of the Maginot Line would not be tested for another eight years. Meanwhile, from December 1932 to December 1933, the foreign situation worsened and four governments wrestled to small purpose with the country's financial and economic problems. The successive premiers were, with one exception, new to their high office. They mostly served in one another's cabinets, for each ministry was largely a reshuffling of the old, and they were leading political figures to the end of the regime. They were all Radicals, except for the eloquent,

Right: *Laval and François-Poncet disembark for yet another Great Power Conference.* **Top right:** *Sennep's prophetic comparison (1930) of the Nazi steamroller and the French wheelchair, with President Doumergue escorting a hospitalised Briand.* **Bottom:** *Radical politicians Chautemps and Daladier*

5

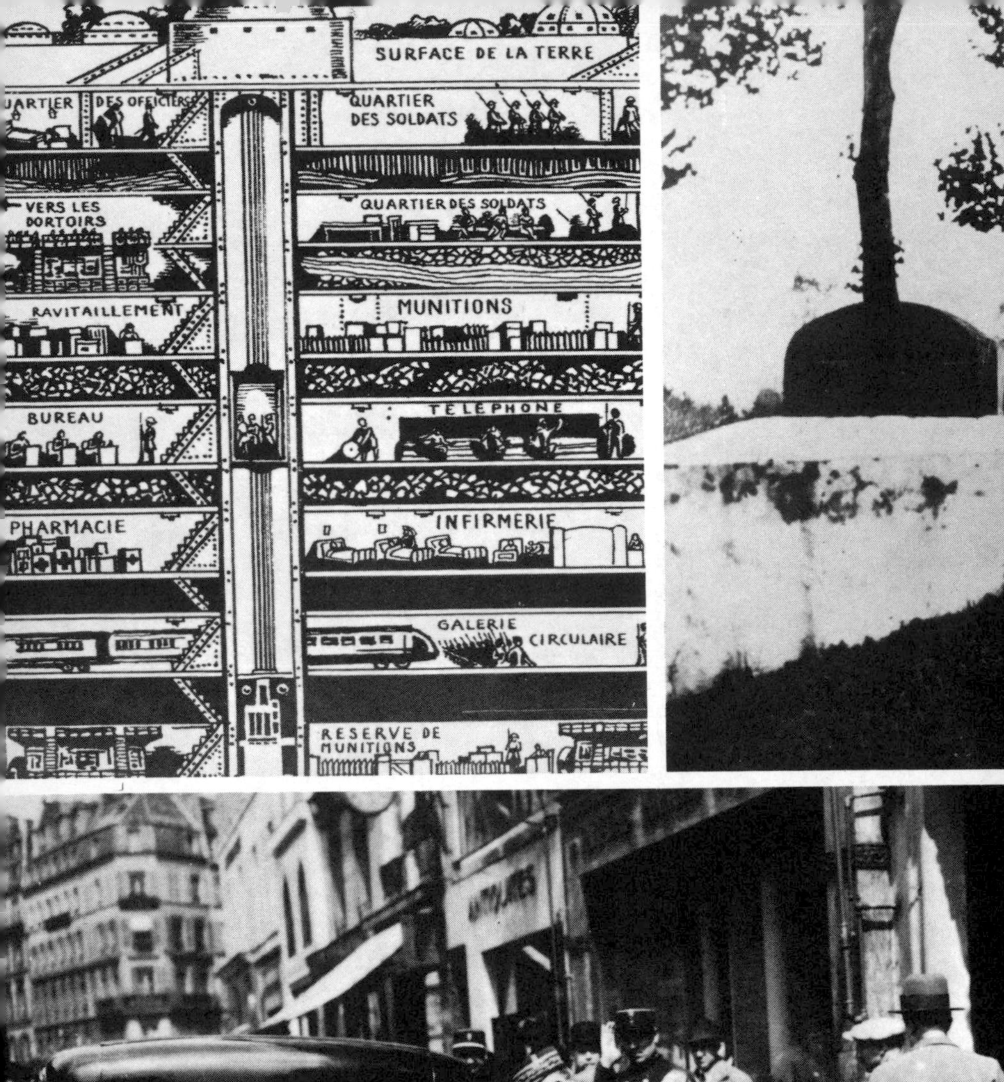
SURFACE DE LA TERRE
UARTIER DES OFFICIERS
QUARTIER DES SOLDATS
VERS LES DORTOIRS
QUARTIER DES SOLDATS
RAVITAILLEMENT
MUNITIONS
BUREAU
TELEPHONE
PHARMACIE
INFIRMERIE
GALERIE CIRCULAIRE
RESERVE DE MUNITIONS

10
S1
163073

white-maned Paul-Boncour, and adept at the party game. But none had the prestige of a Poincaré or the statesman-like qualities so urgently needed and all were hampered by the continued refusal of the Socialists to participate and by their inability to form the Centre groups into a coherent bloc. Paul-Boncour had courage but tended to confuse oratory with action. Daladier, Herriot's rival as Radical party leader, had flair but lacked character – purposeful in looks and manner he was, said his enemies, really only 'a bull with snail's horns'. Chautemps, a disciple of Herriot, was a supple freemason and Sarraut, brother of the director of the well-known provincial newspaper, the *Dépêche de Toulouse,* had been a good Governor-General of Indo-China.

In the spring of 1932 the French economy, apart from agriculture, had taken a turn for the better which persisted until the middle of 1933. But Roosevelt's devaluation of the dollar in March 1933 was a severe blow to France and the other countries still on the gold standard. It was as though France's export prices had increased by twenty-five to thirty per cent. Production again declined, unemployment soared by the end of the year to over a million and, a new disquieting factor, foreign investors were no longer so sure of the franc: for the first time since the mid-twenties gold once again began to leave the country. Agricultural prices continued to fall, especially those of wheat since, as ill-luck would have it, the harvests of 1932 and 1933 were bumper crops, and the government's efforts to bolster them by artificial means were ineffectual. 'A sterile bureaucracy,' it has been said, 'confined itself to vain regulation.' No effort was made to tackle the causes of inefficient farming.

So too no effort was made to reform the financial structure. Harassed and short-lived, the successive governments were too preoccupied by the ever-growing deficit to contemplate radical change. Drastic economies were necessary if the budget was to be balanced and one cabinet after another proposed tax increases and reductions in wages and pensions of state employees and others. Yet, although the cost of living had fallen, the employees, now organised in unions of their own, were at once up in arms. They were supported by the CGT and it was largely union pressure which brought about Paul-Boncour's fall in January 1933. When Daladier in turn proposed to reduce ex-servicemen's pensions they too mobilised in outraged protest. There was a general stampede from the

Top left: *France's defensive outlook, characterised by the Maginot Line, became a dangerous obsession.* ***Bottom:*** *Weygand, who pleaded in vain for the extension of the Line, seen shortly after the assassination of President Doumer in 1932*

call to make sacrifices. The 1933 budget was delayed for six months. At the end of the year, however, Chautemps succeeded in inducing the now weary Chamber to vote a draft budget for 1934. It looked as though there might be a brief period of stability. But this was not to be. In January 1934 a new financial scandal, the Stavisky Affair, burst upon the public and brought a growing anti-parliamentarianism to its menacing climax.

Corruption in high places

Although parliament had been under a cloud during the financial crisis of the mid-twenties, this was a passing phenomenon. There was a rising current of anger with the politicians who failed to remedy France's ills and who presented such a sorry spectacle of seemingly self-seeking incompetence. The governmental machine appeared to be grinding to a halt and French parliamentary government to be a laughing-stock just when dictatorial regimes elsewhere were striding ahead. Discontent manifested itself in the multiplication of leagues and the spread of disorder. Already in November 1931 the noisy, royalist *Camelots du Roi* had been joined by Taittinger's *Jeunesses Patriotes* and the *Croix de Feu* when they broke up a disarmament meeting addressed by Herriot and many figures of international renown. There were several other mainly Right-wing demonstrations in Paris during the next two years. The *Action Française* took a leading part and the *Croix de Feu,* an ex-servicemen's association financed by the perfumer François Coty and another magnate, rapidly gained in importance. On the Left as well as the Right there were men who looked enviously at dictatorial regimes, and at the end of 1933 thirty Socialists, weary of Blum's doctrinaire abstentionism, broke away and founded a Neo-Socialist Party which leaned towards fascism. Meanwhile disorder had spread to the provinces—taxpayers refused to pay increased taxes, veterans demonstrated against reduced pensions, and Communist and other agitators found ready listeners among an increasingly sombre peasantry. In Chartres in March 1933 a new Agrarian Party held a meeting which led to violent clashes and many injuries. Its supporters carried pitchforks.

The Stavisky Affair brought all this disorder to a head, for it seemed to demonstrate that parliament was not merely incompetent but also corrupt.

Serge-Alexandre Stavisky was an elegant swindler whose latest venture collapsed at the end of 1933 leaving him with many million francs worth of bonds issued on the security of Bayonne's municipal pawnshop. A deputy was deeply implicated, the Minister of Colonies had once recommended the bonds as a good investment,

and Stavisky, who had been arrested for fraud in 1927, had been successfully operating ever since on a 'provisional' release which had been extended nineteen times pending trial. The head of the judicial department responsible for these releases was brother-in-law to Chautemps, the Prime Minister. Although the scandal directly involved only a few civil servants and politicians, these revelations were very damaging. Chautemps did his best to make light of the affair and insist that justice must take its course, but this was not easy after 8th January 1934 when Stavisky was found dead in a villa at Chamonix. The *Action Française,* which had already started a campaign against 'the Thieves', now denounced 'the Assassins'. Its charge that Chautemps had ordered Stavisky's murder to prevent further revelations was widely believed. When he unwisely refused a commission of enquiry this was taken as proof of his guilt.

Such a scandal might have been tailor-made for the anti-parliamentary leagues. The *Action Française* denounced the way in which, when people were making economic sacrifices, public savings had been 'available for the colossal swindles of an alien crook'. Parliament was reviled and ridiculed, especially in the Right-wing press – a cartoon in *Le Rire* showed a hostess addressing her servants: 'We have a minister and two deputies coming tonight . . . you will count the spoons'. The leagues organised demonstrations against 'Republican corruption' and after 9th January there was a series of riots in the capital. On the 27th Chautemps resigned. For the first time in the history of the regime a government with a parliamentary majority had bowed to menace from the streets.

Chautemps was succeeded by Daladier whose attempt to form a government of national union failed because the Right refused to co-operate. To ensure Socialist support he dismissed Chiappe, who had been Prefect of Police for seven years and who overtly sympathised with the Right. But Chiappe refused the post in Morocco offered as a consolation. For the Right he became a martyr and his dismissal was the immediate cause of the great demonstrations of 6th February, organised by various Leagues and swelled by indignant crowds. The demonstrators converged on the Place de la Concorde and tried to force their way across the river to the Chamber where Daladier was presenting his cabinet to parliament. They attempted to break through the police cordon protecting the Palais Bourbon. In the five hours' fierce fighting that followed, the police twice fired into the crowd. By the end of the day fifteen people had been killed and more

Left: *The Entente Cordiale – Ramsay MacDonald and Herriot, 1932*

than a thousand injured. Many people thought that there had been a plot to overthrow the regime; but the action of the leagues was unco-ordinated and the *Action Française,* which had always advocated a *coup de force,* was quite unprepared to exploit the situation. Had the Chamber been invaded, there is no knowing what might have happened. As it was, for the first time since the Commune of 1871 blood had been shed in Paris in a bitter surge of anti-parliamentarianism.

On the morrow Daladier resigned, although he had been given a vote of confidence while the riots were in progress. But manifestations continued. On 9th February Communist demonstrations involved further casualties and on the 12th Socialists and Communists for once combined to stage a great demonstration while the unions for the first time successfully organised a general strike. But these were the last serious manifestations. The forces of order had rallied and meanwhile Lebrun had found a new Premier. Once again, as in 1926, a former President of the Republic was summoned to save the situation. The genial septuagenarian Doumergue was fetched from his rural retirement in the south and quickly formed a government of national union which included men of all parties except the Socialists and Communists. The effect was immediate. Confidence was restored and the Chamber, much more scared than in 1926, gave the government still wider powers to legislate by decree.

But the events of 1932-4 were deeply disquieting. The economic crisis had worsened, Germany was becoming more truculently powerful, France's friends in Eastern Europe were beginning to lose confidence in their great ally, public opinion at home was polarised more sharply than ever between Left and Right, and Parliament itself had been horribly discredited. It looked as though France had signally failed to adjust her social and political system to meet the needs of the modern world. Could she still do so before it was too late?

***Right:** 6th February 1934—demonstrators fill the Avenue des Champs-Elysées shortly before the street-fighting began*

Chronology of Events

1918 **11th November:** Germany signs the Armistice at Compiègne.
1919 **28th June:** signature of Treaty of Versailles.
November: Election of the Assembly and victory of the Right-wing *Bloc National.*
1920 **January:** Deschanel elected President against Clemenceau, who resigns. Government of Millerand.
September: Millerand elected President on Deschanel's retirement.
December: Socialist Congress at Tours gives birth to the Communist Party.
1921 **February:** Franco-Polish treaty—first of the alliances with Eastern European states.
1922 **January:** Poincaré becomes Premier and Foreign Minister.
December: conference in London considers Germany's request for a reparations moratorium.
1923 **11th January:** Franco-Belgian occupation of the Ruhr.
27th September: Stresemann announces end of passive resistance.
1924 **16th April:** Germany accepts Dawes Plan recommending French withdrawal from the Ruhr and German reflation.
May: electoral victory of the *Cartel des Gauches.*
June: Millerand resigns, Doumergue elected President. Herriot forms cabinet.
1925 **April:** Herriot is succeeded by Painlevé, thereafter by a 'cascade' of changing governments.
12th April: Abd-el-Krim attacks French-protected Beni Zeroual tribe.
July: evacuation of the Ruhr begins.
October: Locarno agreements include treaty guaranteeing Franco-German and Belgo-German frontiers.
1925 Briand begins seven-year term as Foreign Minister.
1926 **July:** Poincaré's government issues decree-laws to dispel the crisis of the franc.
1928 Military service reduced to one year, followed by decision to build Maginot Line. Poincaré announces devaluation of the franc (June).
27th August: Kellogg Pact signed.
1929 **July:** Poincaré (d. 1934) retires owing to ill-health.
September: Briand proposes European Federal Union.
1930 **May:** Young Plan, reducing scale of German reparations, comes into operation.
June: French evacuation of the Rhineland.
1931 **May:** Doumer defeats Briand in Presidential elections on Doumergue's end of term.
1931 Depression and unemployment become increasingly severe.
1932 **May:** assassination of Doumer; Lebrun becomes President. Electoral success of *Cartel des Gauches*; Herriot's last cabinet is quickly succeeded by five Radical governments in 14 months.
1933 **January-October:** Daladier's government.
1934 **January:** Stavisky financial scandal breaks. Disorder mounts.
6th February: Attempted coup d'état by the Leagues.

***Top:** Advertisement for a bleach—Clemenceau washes out the Kaiser's crimes (left); poster appeals for aid to France's war-stricken regions (centre); President Poincaré visits a steel-mill in Lorraine, September 1919 (right). **Middle** and **bottom:** Caricature of the prickly Poincaré; illuminations on the Eiffel Tower during the Exhibition of Decorative Arts, 1925; and Sennep's cartoon of Briand's proposals for a European Federal Union, 1929: Briand, leaning on the mantelpiece with his hat sporting the stars of the American flag, fails to impress the rest of the cabinet, which includes Barthou (leaning on the back of the sleeping Doumergue's chair), Tardieu (smoking a cigarette), and Painlevé (bouncing on the Republic's knees)*

Les Etats-Unis d'Europe---
J. SENNEP

Index of main people, places, and events

Author's suggestions for further reading

Albrecht-Carrié, R.
A Diplomatic History of Europe since the Congress of Vienna, London, 1958. Chapters X to XII give a useful survey of international politics from 1914 to 1936.

Binion, R.
Defeated Leaders: The Political Fate of Caillaux, Jouvenel, and Tardieu, New York, 1968. A lively sketch of three politicians of the period.

Charvet, P.E.
A Literary History of France, Vol V, London, 1967. Chapters VIII to XI give a vivid account of literary figures and trends between 1914 and 1940.

Hampden-Jackson, J.
Clemenceau and the Third Republic, London, 1946. A very readable biography in the *Teach Yourself History* series.

Jordan, W.M.
Great Britain, France, and the German Problem, 1918-1939, London, 1943. An able analysis of some of the main problems of Anglo-French relations.

La Gorce, P.M.de
The French Army: a military-political history, London, 1963. Chapters 7 to 11 give interesting glimpses of the mood of the army between 1918 and 1934.

Sauvy, A.
Histoire Economique de la France entre les deux guerres, Vols I and II, Paris, 1965 and 1967. The fullest economic study of the period: often highly technical, but full of fascinating detail.

Siegfried, A.
France, a Study in Nationality, Yale, 1930. A classic and witty survey of France's social and political structure.

Weber, E.
Action Française: Royalism and Reaction in Twentieth-century France, Stanford, 1962. A full account of a notable and paradoxical movement.

Library of the 20th Century will include the following titles:

Russia in Revolt
David Floyd
The Second Reich
Harold Kurtz
The Anarchists
Roderick Kedward
Suffragettes International
Trevor Lloyd
War by Time-Table
A.J.P.Taylor
Death of a Generation
Alistair Horne
Suicide of the Empires
Alan Clark
Twilight of the Habsburgs
Z.A.B.Zeman
Early Aviation
Sir Robert Saundby
Birth of the Movies
D.J.Wenden
America Comes of Age
A.E.Campbell
Lenin's Path to Power
G.Katkov and H.Shukman
Weimar Germany
Sefton Delmer
Out of the Lion's Paw
Constantine Fitzgibbon
Japan: The Years of Triumph
Louis Allen
Communism Takes China
C.P.FitzGerald
Black and White in South Africa
G.H.Le May
Woodrow Wilson
E.A.Ions
France: The Insecure Peace
J.P.T.Bury
France: Partial Eclipse
W.Knapp
Mussolini's Italy
E.M.Robertson
The Little Dictators
A.Polonsky
Viva Zapata
L.Bethell
The World Depression
Malcolm Falkus
Stalin's Russia
A.Nove
The Brutal Reich
Donald Watt
The Spanish Civil War
Raymond Carr
Munich: Czech Tragedy
K.G.Robbins

J.P.T.Bury, who was educated at Marlborough and Corpus Christi College, Cambridge, has been a Fellow of Corpus Christi College since 1933. During the war he served in the Ministry of Supply and the Foreign Office Research Department. A University Lecturer in History since 1937, he edited *The Cambridge Historical Journal* (now *The Historical Journal*) for seven years. He has also edited Volume X of the *New Cambridge Modern History* and (with Rohan Butler) six volumes of the First Series of *Documents on British Foreign Policy 1919-1939.* Among his other published works are *France 1814-1940—A History* (fourth ed., 1969) and *Napoleon III and the Second Empire.* He has a book on the career of Gambetta from 1871 to 1877 nearing completion.

J.M.Roberts, General Editor of the *Macdonald Library of the 20th Century,* is Fellow and Tutor in Modern History at Merton College, Oxford. He was also General Editor of Purnell's *History of the 20th Century,* is Joint-Editor of the *English Historical Review,* and author of *Europe 1880-1945* in the Longman's History of Europe. He has been English Editor of the *Larousse Encyclopedia of Modern History,* has reviewed for *The Observer, New Statesman,* and *Spectator,* and given talks on the BBC.

Library of the 20th Century

Editor: Richard Johnson
Executive Editor: Peter Prince
Designed by: Brian Mayers/ Germano Facetti
Design: Henning Boehlke
Research: Germano Facetti/ Evan Davies

Pictures selected from the following sources:

Archives Rencontre 8 12 15 46 82 108 110 120 140
Bibliotheque Nationale Paris 54
Cycling Magazine 111
Rene Dazy 22
Will Dyson/Odhams Ltd 32
M.L.Guaita 113 116
A.Guillaume 10
L'Illustration 28 87 114 118 128
Imperial War Museum 1 146
International Institute for Social History Amsterdam 58
Keystone 110
Kladderadatsch 64 84 100
Library of Congress 124
Lords Gallery 37
Trustees of David Low 44
Musée de La Guerre Paris Cover
Nebelspalter 93 96
Philadelphia Museum of Art 17
Popperfoto 63 72 76 77 78 122 142
Radio Times Hulton 88
Simplicissimus 59 65
Snark International 20 38 40 57 133 134
Suddeutscher Verlag 6 15 31 67 102 130 138 139
Jules Tallandier 48
United Press International 141
Roger Viollet 4 6 14 24 26 31 34 43 51 60 70 74 79 80 85 91 99 104 127 145 146 147 152

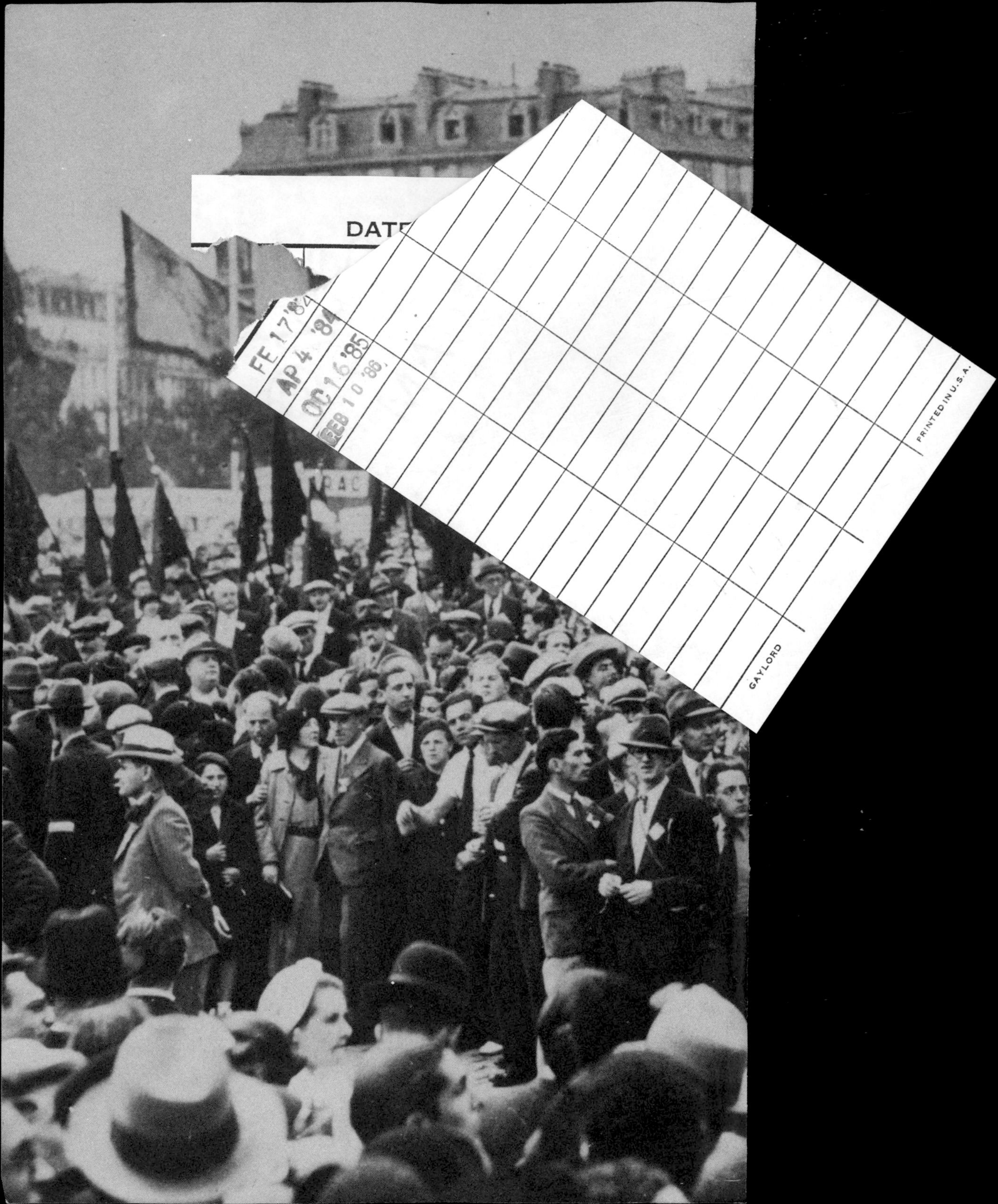